ANATOMY AND BALLET

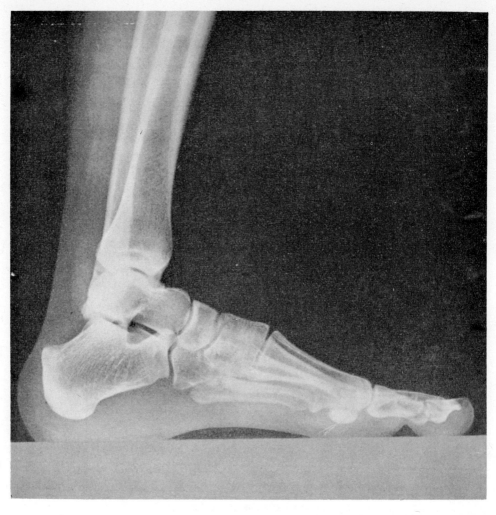

X-RAY OF DANCER'S FOOT SEEN FROM INNER SIDE
AND BEARING FULL WEIGHT OF BODY

Compare with Fig. 28B which shows the same foot in a different position.

ANATOMY AND BALLET

A Handbook for Teachers of Ballet

by
CELIA SPARGER

FOREWORD BY S. L. HIGGS, F.R.C.S.

INTRODUCTION BY DAME NINETTE DE VALOIS, D.B.E.

FIFTH EDITION

*With 43 X-ray and other photographs
and 51 drawings*

THEATRE ARTS BOOKS
NEW YORK

FIRST PUBLISHED 1949
BY A. AND C. BLACK (PUBLISHERS) LTD
35 BEDFORD ROW, LONDON WC1R 4JH

SECOND EDITION 1952
THIRD EDITION 1960
FOURTH EDITION, REVISED AND ENLARGED, 1965
FIFTH EDITION 1970
© 1970 CELIA SPARGER

ISBN: 0-7136-1080-8

To

MARGARET CRASKE

FROM WHOM THE AUTHOR WAS
FORTUNATE ENOUGH TO RECEIVE
HER TRAINING IN BALLET TECHNIQUE

ACKNOWLEDGMENTS

Grateful acknowledgment is made to W. Heffer & Sons, Ltd., for permission to use Figs. 1 and 2 from *Surface and Radiological Anatomy* by A. B. Appleton, W. J. Hamilton and I. C. C. Tchaperoff, and to Edward Arnold Ltd., for Figs. 23, 24 and 25, from *Anatomy and Physiology*, 2nd edition, by C. F. V. Smout and R. J. S. McDowall. Thanks are also due to Mr. Philip Wiles, F.R.C.S., and Messrs. J. & A. Churchill Ltd., for allowing me to use Fig. 50 from *Essentials of Orthopaedics*, and to the students of the Royal Academy of Dancing and of the Royal Ballet School who posed for Figs. 45, 47, 48, 49 and 52.

And illustratons on pp. 55 and 59 have been drawn by Miss Helen Wilson and Patrick Furse respectively, and those on pp. 68, 69 and 86 by Peter Revitt, to all three of whom I offer my thanks.

First published in the United States, 1971
by Theatre Arts Books
153 Waverly Place, New York, 10014

REPRINTED 1972, 1976, 1978, 1982

Printed in Great Britain by The Whitefriars Press Ltd, Tonbridge

CONTENTS

		PAGE
	FOREWORD	6
	INTRODUCTION	7
	PREFACE TO THE FOURTH EDITION	7
	PREFACE TO THE FIRST EDITION	8

CHAPTER

I. INTRODUCTORY: *The Skeleton* — 9

II. THE SPINE — 17
Structure—curves—weak spots—movements in each region—how produced

III. THORAX AND SHOULDER GIRDLE — 20
Structure—movements in shoulder joint—forearm and hand—effect of stiffness in shoulder joint on spine and ports de bras—breathing—contracted chest muscles—influence on breathing

IV. PELVIS AND HIP JOINT — 22
Structure—sacro-iliac joint—shape of femur and its influence on "knock-knees"—normal limit of hip movements

V. MOVEMENTS OF SPINE AND HIPS — 24
Movement of spine direct and indirect—in développé and arabesque—influence on posture of tilt of pelvis

VI. THE KNEE JOINT — 29
Structure and normal movements—increased movement in ronds-de-jambe—locking of knee in "pulling up thighs"

VII. THE FOOT — 32
Structure—visible bony points—"rolling"—arches

VIII. LIGAMENTS OF FOOT AND ANKLE JOINT — 36
Importance of ligaments—flat foot v. dancer's foot

IX. MOVEMENTS OF THE FOOT AND ANKLE JOINT — 38
Normal movements—sickle in and out—action of muscles in movement

X. THE FOOT IN ORDER AND DISORDER — 42
Importance of correct standing—turning out from hips—use of muscles of sole of foot—soft v. blocked shoes

XI. MUSCLES IN POSTURE AND "PLACING" — 46
Posture a function of Central Nervous System—ballet a method of educating C.N.S.

XII. COMMON FAULTS — 50
Anatomical reasons for some common faults at the "barre"

XIII. STRESSES AND STRAINS — 63

XIV. QUESTIONS AND ANSWERS — 73

BOOKS RECOMMENDED — 96

FOREWORD

By S. L. HIGGS, M.A., M.B., B.CH. (CANTAB.), F.R.C.S. (ENG.)
Formerly Consulting Orthopaedic Surgeon, St. Bartholomew's Hospital

A book on Anatomy written for the ballet dancer will surely be welcome.

Ballet is an expression of the perfect functioning of limbs and joints, and a basic knowledge of the underlying mechanism must be of value especially to those who have to select, train and supervise students.

This book is written by one who has studied the problems of anatomy and function in their relation to physical training, physiotherapy and the ballet, and who is qualified to write authoritatively of all three—perhaps a unique distinction.

I have known Miss Sparger for many years and I have always attributed her remarkable skill in treating children with deformities and postural defects to her thorough understanding of muscle control and poise acquired through her ballet experience.

From my experience as an orthopaedic surgeon I have come to the conclusion that it is very desirable that those who have the responsibility of selecting students for training for ballet should have a sound knowledge of normal anatomy and abnormal physical conditions. Without this, children of unsuitable physique may be accepted with perhaps harmful results to themselves, and inevitable disappointment to all concerned. I am, unfortunately, familiar with the harmful results of ballet training which can lead to the aggravation of minor defects in children who, in the first place, were unsuitable, and also with disorders which have arisen through the unwise or perhaps unskilled application of the technique of training And yet, when well applied to selected children, the training and profession of a ballet dancer can lead to physical perfection.

It is important that teachers should be well versed in the matters so clearly set out in this book if un-physiological strains in young children are to be avoided. The ordinary academic text-books of anatomy are of little value. It is the anatomy of movement in ballet which is required and Miss Sparger's book provides this.

INTRODUCTION

By NINETTE DE VALOIS, D.B.E.

I can welcome this book as a future standard work for the bookshelf of the teacher and the older student. The teaching of ballet has many problems, and the teacher finds that to impart this art is a fascinating and ever-changing form of work. Observation is the keynote after the teacher has received his fundamental training. But observation has a habit of sometimes turning into a long sustained question mark. It is at this point that I strongly feel that this book will be able to help, for it is written by someone who loves the ballet and has taken the trouble to study and execute our exercises. She has now taken us into a world behind the scene of movement in relation to the dance. It is in this world that we can see how much we do ask of our pupils, and can find a helpful answer to some of our problems.

PREFACE TO THE FOURTH EDITION

This new edition has been substantially enlarged principally by the addition of text and illustrations from my book *Ballet Physique* which is now no longer in print. Chapter XIII, Stresses and Strains, is a new chapter embodying a good deal from my other book and in Chapter XIV, Questions and Answers, several of the Questions have been dealt with at greater length and illustrated by X-rays, photographs and drawings previously in *Ballet Physique*.

As recorded in prefaces in earlier editions I am grateful to Miss Carolyn Parks, President of The Academy of Ballet, San Francisco, who suggested some of the questions, and to the Editor of *Dance Magazine*, New York, which first published these with my answers.

1965   *C. S.*

PREFACE TO THE FIFTH EDITION

In this edition certain anatomical terms, which had previously been retained as being clearer to the lay reader, have been brought into line with those now used in conformity with the latest edition of the *Nomine Anatomica* as revised by the International Nomenclature Committee.

This has seemed desirable in order to avoid confusion for candidates taking the Fellowship Examination in Ballet held by at least one of the Examining bodies in the U.K. and abroad, and which includes a paper on Anatomy, a practice which we may hope will soon be general.

I have to thank Professor R. de C. H. Saunders, Head of the Anatomy Department of Dalhousie University, Halifax, Nova Scotia, Canada, for his advice on the subject and for his detailed scrutiny of the text of this book.

1969   *C. S.*

PREFACE TO THE FIRST EDITION

The origin of this book was a request from the Cecchetti Society for an anatomy syllabus on which to examine candidates for their Teacher's Diploma. It then became obvious that the prior need was for a text-book on which such a syllabus could be based. Books on anatomy are many and valuable and I am indebted to them for much of my material, but they are written for specialists and go too far in most directions, whilst at the same time they do not touch upon the problems of movement which are peculiar to ballet.

Those great teachers who are engaged in training artist-dancers need no text-book. In their own non-scientific language, they have profound understanding of the movements of the body, and of the tremendous power of ballet technique for good or ill. It is to the young and less experienced teachers, those dealing with children of varying ability and every shape and size, and from whom I have had many requests for guidance, that with some diffidence, I offer this book.

It must be understood that anatomy deals solely with the structure and working of the body. It is unaffected by the differences in style and in methods of teaching which characterise the different Schools in the ballet world; therefore, although my own initiation was through the Cecchetti Method, the subject-matter dealt with here will be found to be common to all systems, and will, I hope, be of use to all teachers, of whatever school of thought. Moreover, although for the sake of simplicity I have regarded both teacher and dancer as female, there is nothing except the use of the foot in *pointe* work which does not apply equally to the male.

My grateful thanks are due to Mr. Ross Bloom, B.Sc., M.B., B.S., F.R.C.S., who read the anatomy sections with a critical eye; to Diana Barker, Laura Wilson and others who performed a like service from the point of view of the teacher of ballet; and to Rosamond Mathers who, knowing nothing of either subject, made many valuable suggestions in reading the proofs. To Mr. Philip Wiles, M.S., F.R.C.S., I owe the untying of some of the many knots with which the science and the art of movement are bound.

I cannot express too highly my appreciation of the interest and enthusiasm shown by Peggy van Praagh and by Elaine Fifield, Anne Heaton and Sheilah O'Reilly, who in the midst of a busy season generously gave their time to posing for X-rays and photographs; nor to Mr. D. Stevenson Clark and Mr. A. S. Dilling of Ilford Limited for their skill in securing these, and for their patience and courtesy throughout.

To Eric M. Agnew, who forsook paint and canvas to draw the illustrations, bringing to them an uncommon combination of artistry, knowledge of anatomy and understanding of ballet technique, I offer my deepest thanks.

Lastly it gives me great pleasure to put on record here my gratitude to Gwen, under whose hospitable roof in Cornwall this book was both begun and finished.

C. S.

CHAPTER I

INTRODUCTORY

When a young aspirant elects to become a ballerina her guardians may decide that she shall take her training in England, France, Italy, Russia, Sweden, Australia, China or America. Whatever is the ultimate choice (not necessarily limited even to these countries) one thing is certain, that her first and last lessons will begin with *pliés* at the *barre* and continue through a series of *barre* exercises, repeated in the centre, and finishing with *changements de pieds* or similar movements of elevation. The details of the lesson will vary according to the teacher and her allegiance to one school of thought or another, but the essentials will never vary. Whatever may be the vocal language in which the lesson is conducted, the language of the body will be the same *pliés*, *grand battements*, *battements tendus*, *développés*, etc. This is the alphabet of ballet, from which words and then sentences are constructed. It is the possession of this alphabet which distinguishes ballet dancing from any other, and it has been used for some 200 years as the foundation for that training which produces ultimately the beauty of movement, strength, endurance, poise, agility and speed unequalled in any other system.

What is the origin of this remarkable system? It is not easy to say. All that we know is that, as in any tradition, it has been handed down for generations, by great teachers, whose names are landmarks: Noverre, Blassis, Johanssen, Cecchetti. The teacher of today inherits their work. The dancer, to the last day of her career, uses their fundamental technical exercises at the barre for her daily practice. No others can take their place.

What is the secret of this technique? Did those great teachers first study the anatomy of the body and then decide how to utilise this knowledge? The answer would most certainly be " No ". Undoubtedly they used first and foremost that instinct which is the artist's, and arrived at the truth because they were artists. Some, perhaps, may have pursued later the scientific *raison d'être* for the exercises they created, but probably most were content to follow the inspiration of their eye and that unerring sense of line and form which guided them and led them to the results they sought.

Why then should the modern teacher feel the need for the study of anatomy? For two reasons. Firstly, it is a sad but undeniable fact that when anything that is rare and precious becomes too easy of access, it is in danger of losing something in the process. Whereas at one time the few, the very few carefully selected, physically perfect and gifted children were chosen for initiation into the almost secret and almost sacred Schools of Ballet, and were taught by masters whose life was a dedication to the Art of Dancing and the Art of Teaching, handing on its secrets by demonstration, word of mouth, rare engravings and precious manuscripts; now instead, we have the printed word, the camera, the cinema and the open class. The barriers are down. Ballet has become the property of the masses. So that today, the teacher does not deal with a few selected pupils, vocational and devoted, but with large classes of children. Our aspiring ballerina may be amongst them, but there may also be many with neither the physique nor the gift for a stage career, but nevertheless eager to work and gaining great benefit from some ballet training. These children frequently have minor physical variations for which allowances must be made and for which some understanding of the structure of the body is essential.

Then there is a second interesting development in the teaching of ballet which is the natural outcome of its popularity and in line with the trend of things in other directions, that is, the very high standard which is now required even from the corps-de-ballet. The entire corps-de-ballet in these days is often required to perform movements and steps which in former times would have been regarded as ballerina work. Moreover, many movements not purely traditional or classical are introduced into modern ballets which require a degree of training not even reached perhaps by former ballerinas. This is today a matter of routine, and the modern teacher needs a very watchful eye, good judgment and some knowledge of anatomy in pressing forward such work on her young students.

In presenting the study of anatomy to teachers of ballet, it is not easy to decide where to begin, and, more especially, how far to go. Anatomy is a very large subject and it is a science. Dancing is an art. The scientist has knowledge of the living body; the artist of the moving body. The dancer's knowledge of the moving body is often more detailed and profound than anything to be found in science, but she has not the language in which to express it. She knows by feeling, and by experience within her own body what the scientist knows by study from the outside. It would be a loss should she try to substitute the one for the other. Her eye and her instinct are her strength, and therefore her study of anatomy should be in such a form that these are reinforced, but not replaced, by a more academic approach. So it is with the painter and sculptor.

Curiously enough, anatomy seems to suggest to most people the study of muscles. Actually for the teacher of ballet this is of very little importance, for the simple reason that ballet has its own technique of definite and exact movements. If *these movements are performed correctly the correct muscles will work*. If the movement is not performed correctly, wrong muscles will come into play. A faulty movement is a faulty movement, no matter what muscles have produced it. The dancer cannot begin by trying to find out which muscles to use. The right effort will eventually ensure right muscle work. The art of the teacher is to call forth this effort, when muscles will take care of themselves; which is fortunate, for the study of muscles in action is but half explored and needs many years of detailed arduous study for its understanding. So the teacher's real task is to go deeper, in fact to the skeleton itself, to the joints, the bones, the bony structure of the body. See the moving body as a moving skeleton and very little more is needed. For the most part, that will be the approach in this book. In the foot only will greater detail be given, since it is used in a highly specialised manner, and is subject to misuse and abuse not operating elsewhere. Beyond that, however, our excursions into the world of the science of movement will be confined to a simple understanding of the bony structure of the body, and the effects upon it of the movements which form the foundation of the technique of ballet.

Names and technical terms are not in themselves important. Do not be frightened by them; they are the language of anatomy and students who, having digested this small book, wish to pursue the subject further, will find themselves at sea if they do not recognise the terms employed in larger text-books. Therefore as a beginning study the illustrations of the skeleton, with the tabulation of the names of the various parts, and memorise some definitions of structures which bind, separate or protect it.

The " axial skeleton " is composed of the bones of the head, neck and trunk, whilst the bones of the limbs are termed the " appendicular skeleton ". These latter are in pairs and form the appendages to the main trunk.

Axial Skeleton:

The *spinal or vertebral column* is of importance and should be noted specially. It is constructed of a series of irregular shaped bones called Vertebrae:

    7 cervical vertebrae form the neck.
    12 thoracic vertebrae form (with the ribs) the chest cavity.
    5 lumbar vertebrae form the hollow of the back.
    5 sacral vertebrae fused into one bone form the sacrum.
    4 coccygeal vertebrae fused into one bone form the coccyx.

Sternum or *Breast Bone,* divided into 3 parts:

    Manubrium.   Body.   Xiphoid Process.

Ribs:

    7 pairs attached to vertebrae behind and sternum in front.
    3 pairs attached to vertebrae behind and joined by cartilage to each other in front.
    2 pairs attached behind to vertebrae and free in front (floating ribs).

Appendicular Skeleton, consists of pairs of bones:

    Clavicle or collar bone.
    Scapula or shoulder blade.
    Humerus or upper arm.
    Radius and ulna or forearm.
    8 Carpal bones or wrist.
    5 Metacarpal bones or palm.
    14 Phalanges or fingers.

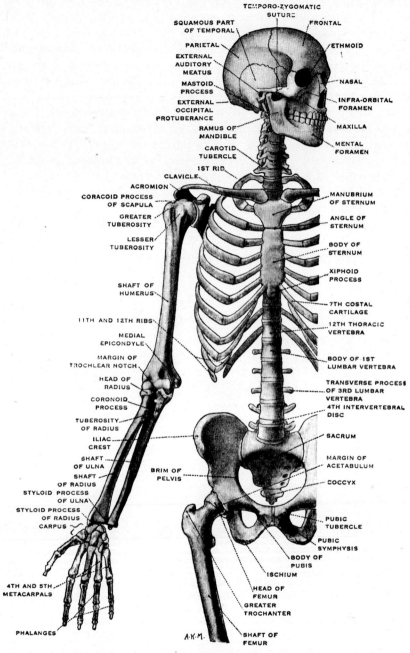

Fig. 1. THE SKELETON, FRONT VIEW
These illustrations have been chosen for their clarity.
The lower limbs will be found elsewhere

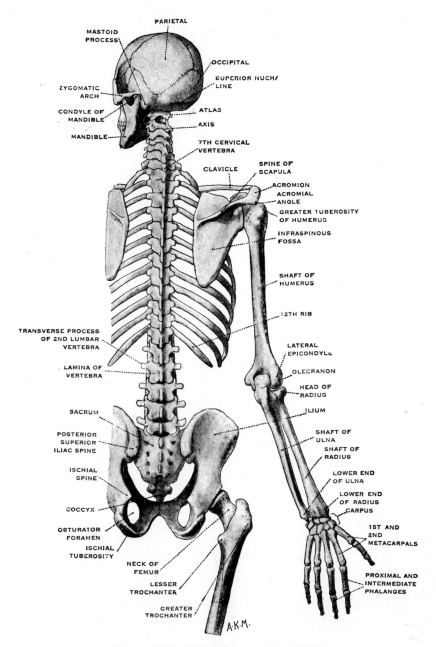

Fig. 2. THE SKELETON, BACK VIEW

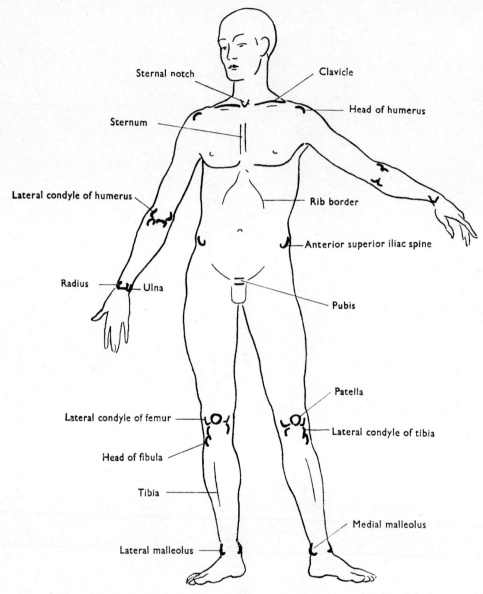

Fig. 3. BONY POINTS WHICH CAN BE SEEN ON, OR FELT NEAR,
THE SURFACE OF THE BODY

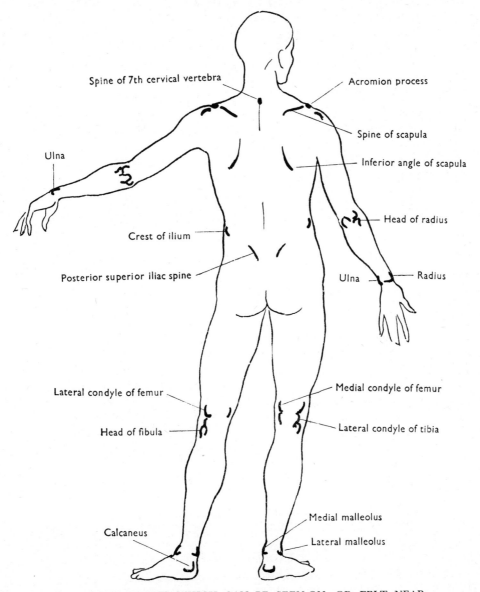

Spine of 7th cervical vertebra

Acromion process

Spine of scapula

Inferior angle of scapula

Ulna

Head of radius

Crest of ilium

Posterior superior iliac spine

Ulna

Radius

Lateral condyle of femur

Medial condyle of femur

Head of fibula

Lateral condyle of tibia

Calcaneus

Medial malleolus

Lateral malleolus

Fig. 4. BONY POINTS WHICH CAN BE SEEN ON, OR FELT NEAR,
THE SURFACE OF THE BODY

Below. Os innominatum or hip bone, divided into:

Ilium ⎫
Ischium ⎬ Two sides with sacrum and coccyx forming the pelvis.
Pubis ⎭

Femur or thigh.
Tibia or shin ⎫
Fibula or brooch bone ⎬ Leg.

Patella or knee cap.
7 Tarsal or ankle bones.
5 Metatarsal or foot bones.
14 Phalanges or toes.

Bone and Joint Characteristics:

Articular surface:	Part of a bone shaped to receive the corresponding part of another bone.
Articulation:	Bone surfaces placed together to form a joint.
Process:	A projection.
Spine:	A sharp projection.
Tubercle:	A roughened protuberance.
Tuberosity:	A rounded end of a protuberance.
Condyle:	Enlarged end of the bone.
Epicondyle:	Projection on a condyle
Ligament:	Bands of tissue binding bones together, thus forming a joint. Can be stretched, but if unduly, will not then return to original length.
Capsule:	Ligamentous tissue enclosing a joint.

Cartilage: Tough elastic substance or gristle used:

(*a*) to line joint surfaces and so facilitate easy gliding of one surface over the other, e.g. knee;

(*b*) or as a junction of bone to bone where resiliency is required, as in ribs to sternum;

(*c*) shock absorber as in spine where bones are separated by discs of cartilage.

Flexion:	Bending, reducing length.
Extension:	Straightening, increasing length.
Rotation:	Twisting.
Abduction:	Movement away from mid-line of body.
Adduction:	Movement towards mid-line of body.
Lateral:	Outer side or further from midline of body.
Medial:	Inner side or nearer to midline of body.
Distal:	Farthest from.
Proximal:	Nearest to.

Before going farther, take a pencil and paper and learn the shape and positions of the bones of the skeleton by drawing them. The eye and the pencil should be the dancer's memory. Follow this method throughout the book. Draw, draw, draw.

CHAPTER II

THE SPINE

The spine is composed of thirty-three irregular shaped bones, but with the exception of the first and second (*atlas* and *axis*) they have certain similarities. The bony mass of each vertebra is termed the *body*. From the body are two projections, the *pedicles*. These continue into two thin blades of bone called *laminae* and the two laminae unite into the prominent spine, the tips of which can be seen at intervals down the back. The position of these *spinous processes*, as they are called, is responsible to some extent for the type of movement which can be obtained in the spine and which will be discussed later. For the moment, it should be noted that in the neck they project backwards and slightly downwards, in the thorax their position is much more oblique and in the lumbar region they are nearly horizontal. In the neck they are short, in the thorax longer and sharper and in the lumbar broad and short. Many of the spinous processes can be seen when the body is bent downward, but the 7th cervical, known as the *vertebra prominens*, can be seen in the upright position, as can, in some people, the 6th cervical and 1st thoracic.

At the junction of the pedicle and lamina there is a lateral or *transverse process* to which the ribs are attached, and above and below on each transverse process is a smooth facet which forms the articulation with the vertebra above and below, whilst blood vessels and nerves pass through the hole or *foramen* formed by the pedicles and transverse processes. Through the large foramen in the centre, formed by the bodies of the vertebrae and their projections, passes the spinal cord, the nerve centre from the brain to the muscles and organs of the entire body.

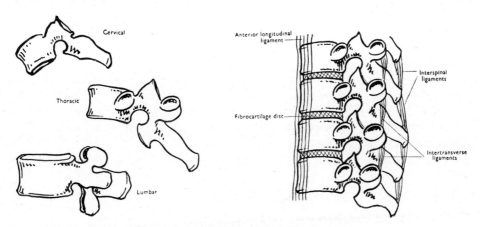

Fig. 5. VERTEBRAE AND LIGAMENTS

Two vertebrae differ from the rest—they are the 1st (*atlas*) and the 2nd (*axis*). The atlas has no body but forms a ring of bone. It articulates with the base of the skull.

The axis is distinguished by a protuberance, the odontoid peg or dens which passes through the ring of the atlas and articulates with a facet on it. Bands of ligaments connect both vertebrae to the base of the skull. It is this arrangement of the vertebrae in this region that enables the head to be held easily, without stiffening the neck muscles, and to perform certain small movements independently of the rest of the neck.

The vertebrae of the spinal column are connected by ligaments and are separated from each other by a disc of spongy elastic cartilage which acts as a shock absorber. These discs vary in shape and thickness and so help in forming the curves of the spine. Thus in the cervical or neck region they are thicker in front than behind,* in the thoracic or chest region, thinner in front than behind, and in the lumbar, as in the cervical, thicker in front. The discs also prevent friction between the bodies of the vertebrae.

Down the whole length of the spine are a series of connecting ligaments. The spinous processes and laminae are connected firmly one to the other below, and the transverse processes less strongly, while the bodies of the vertebrae are united by longitudinal ligaments both in front and behind.

It will be seen, therefore, that it is almost impossible by movement alone to displace a vertebra. (The so-called "bone out of place" is most likely to be a spasm in the adjoining muscles holding a small area of the spine in a fixed position, or a slight misplacement of the discs mentioned above may sometimes occur between two vertebrae, most frequently in the lumbar region.)

The spine has three major curves. These serve, with the help of the inter-vertebral discs, to absorb shock. The degree of each curve varies a good deal in individuals and gives the ultimate shape to the torso. Any permanent alteration in one curve will affect the curves above or below. Thus a flattening of the thoracic curve will plane out the cervical and lumbar. A decrease in the lumbar curve automatically flattens that of the thoracic region; conversely, an increased lumbar curve, a "hollow back", results in a rounded thorax.

The weight of the body passes through the bodies of the vertebrae. As each curve merges into the next, there is a slight weakening of the weight-bearing capacity and so it is that the thoracic curve is apt to increase at the level of the 11th or 12th dorsal vertebrae with age or fatigue, giving the familiar picture of "round back". At the junction of the 5th lumbar vertebra with the sacrum there is another weak spot, and this region of the spine is peculiarly susceptible to muscular strain.

---

* Note here and throughout, "in front" signifies as seen from the front view of the body "behind" as seen looking at the spine from the back.

Movement of Spine

The spinal column moves, not as a whole, but in segments, the vertebrae gliding and turning upon each other. The degree of movement possible depends on the original shape of the whole, the length of the ligaments and the flexibility of the muscles producing the movement. These may not necessarily be in the spine itself. For example, everyone is familiar with the pull of the hamstring muscles at the back of the thigh, which, if tight, will prevent forward bending in the lumbar region of the back.

In the neck, all movements are free and unimpeded. Tilting up of the chin and a certain degree of dropping forward can (and should) take place in the atlas-axis-occiput joints alone. In the thoracic region turning and side-bending are free, back bending is very limited. Even in an acrobatic back bend this region scarcely moves for, as can be seen in the illustrations, the spinous processes are arranged in a downward and oblique direction and would quickly impinge on each other if any great degree of backward movement were possible. In the lumbar region all movements are free except rotation, i.e. twisting from side to side, which is practically absent.

The spine can be moved in two ways, one by the direct effort of bending, turning or twisting, and the other by tilting the pelvis. Therefore it is necessary to become familiar with the pelvis and hip joint before discussing these further; but even before that, the influence of the shoulder girdle must be understood.

CHAPTER III

THORAX AND SHOULDER GIRDLE

Looking at the illustration of the skeleton it can be seen that the thorax consists of twelve pairs of ribs, attached behind to the vertebrae, whilst in front, seven pairs articulate with the body of the sternum and three merge into each other by a cartilaginous union, leaving the last two pairs free in front—floating, as they are often called. The upper seven ribs are joined to the sternum by cartilage, thus giving resiliency to the fixed portion of the thorax, whilst the arrangement of the lower ribs ensures both resiliency and flexibility to the cavity as a whole.

The *scapulae* or shoulder blades lie upon the upper ribs and, being freely movable, are not attached to them; but a ridge of bone across the upper end, known as the *spine of the scapula*, ends in a prominent process, the *acromion*, which articulates with the clavicle. This is often visible and can always be felt.

The *clavicle* lies across the upper thorax, almost horizontally, avoiding contact with the ribs by the familiar curve which can be seen just before it articulates at its inner end with the manubrium of the sternum. There is some movement at the shoulder end, but only a slight gliding and rotation at the sternal end, and therefore it follows that the scapula and clavicle must work as one unit. Their movement is, however, complicated by that of the humerus.

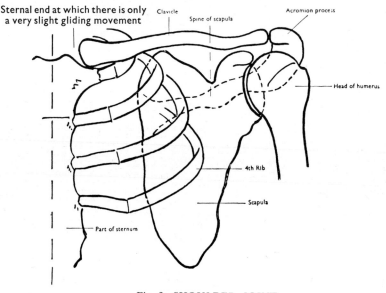

Fig. 6. SHOULDER JOINT

20

The *humerus* articulates with the scapula by means of a shallow fossa below the acromion process. It is known as the *glenoid fossa* and, with the rounded end of the humerus, forms a ball and socket structure similar to that of the hip but not so deep. As in the hip joint, it is enclosed in a capsule and strengthened by ligaments crossing the joint in front and behind.

Raising of the arm as far as shoulder level takes place in the shoulder joint alone, but these three bones, the scapula, clavicle and humerus, are involved in all movements of the arms *above* shoulder height. The forearm and hand work independently.

The forearm consists of *ulna* and *radius*, the former articulating with the lower end of the humerus and the latter forming the greater part of the wrist joint. In the wrist are eight *carpal* bones, in the hand five *metacarpals* and in the fingers fourteen *phalanges*. Their shape and position can be readily seen in Figs. 1 and 2, but since in dancing the arms form an extremely important but not damageable part of the body, their structure should be visualised but need not be learnt in detail. The shoulder girdle, however, plays a definite part in adding to the troubles of the dancer, for if there is any stiffness in it, if the arms cannot be raised overhead fully, without strain, the movement will then be transferred to the spine and the result will be an unpleasing picture of hollow or sway back and poking head (with correspondingly bad *ports-de-bras*). Stiffness may be confined to the shoulder joint alone, or may be brought about by contracted chest muscles; this contraction results in bad posture and restricted breathing; conversely, shallow breathing, from whatever cause, may produce poor posture. The value of breathing deeply is not so much the effect on the lungs as the mobilising effect of the chest wall and even of the spine. In a freely flexible thorax breathing will take care of itself and alternatively a flexible thorax and shoulder girdle will aid full and natural breathing; contracted chest muscles will restrict the movements of the shoulder girdle, which in turn impedes the movements of the thoracic spine. Then follow alterations in the position of the lumbar spine and pelvic girdle. And so, to the pelvis and hip joint.

CHAPTER IV

PELVIS AND HIP JOINT

The shape of the *sacrum* and *coccyx* can be seen in the illustration. The sacrum articulates on either side with the hip bones and forms with them the basin-like structure known as the *pelvis*. The hip or *innominate* bone consists of three bones fused together, the *ilium, ischium* and *pubis*. There is an important articulation between the sacrum and ilium known as the *sacro-iliac joint*. Strong ligaments cross this joint from sacrum to ilium. There is normally a little give between the bones but only in childbirth is there any appreciable yielding. Should anything more develop through strain, often due to alterations in the normal curves of the spine, considerable pain and inconvenience may arise. Reference will again be made to this joint shortly.

The recognisable landmarks of the pelvis are the crest of the ilium, the anterior and posterior superior iliac spines.

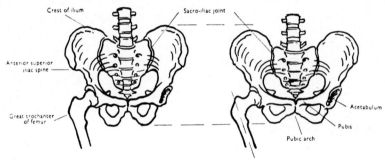

Fig. 7. MALE PELVIS.　　FEMALE PELVIS. (Note the more oval shape)

In sitting, the body rests on the ischial tuberosities, just above which, on either side, is a cup-shaped cavity that receives the head of the femur or thigh bone and is known as the *acetabulum*.

The *femur* has a large rounded head, which fits the deep cup or acetabulum of the ilium in ball and socket formation, so forming the hip joint. Below this rounded head is a short shaft of bone called the neck of the femur. (This is the usual site of a fracture of the thigh, more especially in elderly people.) The junction of the neck and the long shaft of the bone is strengthened by a large bony mass or *trochanter*, and it is at this junction that the position of the knees are determined, for, according to the angle formed here, so will the knees meet. Normally the angle is about 125° in the male, somewhat less in the female. Should the angle be less than this, the shaft of the femur will slope inwards and the lower ends meet too closely, giving the familiar shape seen more often in girls than boys, and known as "knock-knees".

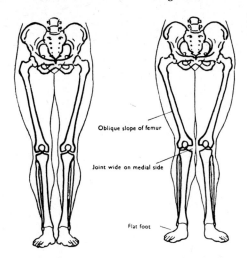

Fig. 8.
KNOCK-KNEES

Oblique slope of femur

Joint wide on medial side

Flat foot

The hip joint is enclosed in a capsule lined with lubricating membrane. In front, this capsule has a thickened band known as the Y-shaped ligament of Bigelow or ilio-femoral ligament. It is this ligament, far more than muscles, which controls the degree of movement possible in the hip, and limits what would otherwise be very free movement in the joint.

Other strong bands of ligaments hold the head within the acetabulum and connect the upper end of the femur to the pubis and ischium.

All movements are free in the hip joint but are not as big in range as might be expected, since the Y-shaped ligament limits them. Quite soon they are transferred to the pelvis and thence to the spine. We will therefore retrace our steps and again consider the movements of the spine, this time in conjunction with the pelvis and hip joint.

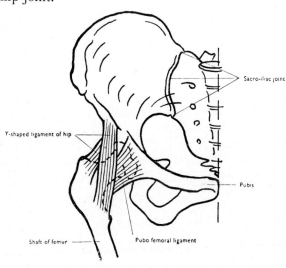

Fig. 9.
Y-SHAPED
LIGAMENT
OF HIP

Sacro-iliac joint

Y-shaped ligament of hip

Pubis

Shaft of femur

Pubo femoral ligament

CHAPTER V

MOVEMENTS OF SPINE AND HIPS

We have already mentioned that there are two ways of obtaining movement in the spine, one by direct action and the other by tilting the pelvis.

When the body weight is on both hips, as in sitting, the spine can be bent forward throughout its whole length. Backward bending, however, occurs in the lumbar and cervical regions and in a very slight degree only in the thoracic region (restricted by the slope of the spinous processes behind and the limited expansion of the ribs in front). Side-bending takes place throughout the spine, but rotation is most free in the upper thoracic and cervical area and is practically absent in the lumbar. It is obvious, however, that in the standing position there is a much bigger range of movement in all directions, for then the pelvis can take part, rolling forward and backward on the hip joints (in flexion and extension of the spine), twisting from side to side (in rotary movements of the body), and tilting from side to side (in side-bending of the body).

This participation of the pelvis and hip joints in movements of the spine is greatly increased when the weight of the body is on one leg only, especially in all bending and rotation movements when it is, in fact, impossible to localise the movement to the spine itself.

There is one other movement in the spinal column which dancers especially need to use; that of the balancing of the head at the axis-atlas-occiput articulations. This should be a free movement practically independent of the cervical spine. It is small and quickly inhibited by any tension in the neck muscles but its correct use makes the difference between a delicate but free use of the head and one stiff and restricted.

So much for the movements of the spine by direct effort. These same movements can all be produced, but indirectly and in a much smaller range, through leg movements originating in the hip joint.

The movements of the hip joint are much more limited than they appear, Pure hip movement forward stops at about 60°, sideways at 40° and backward at 15°.

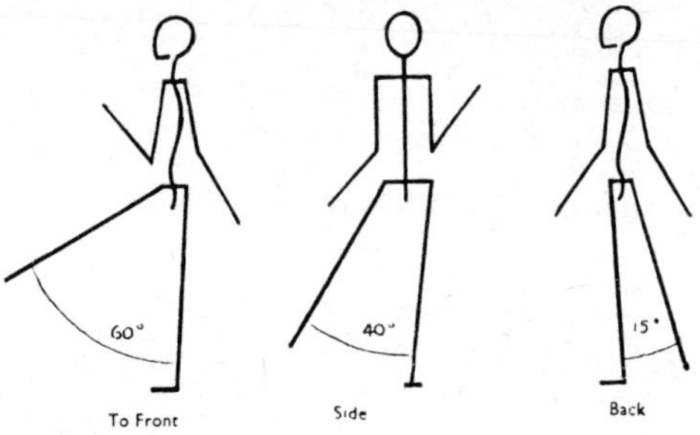

Fig. 10. SHOWING THE LIMITATION OF PURE HIP MOVEMENT IN AN AVERAGE PERSON

60° To Front   40° Side   15° Back

Fig. 11.
DÉVELOPPÉ À LA SECONDE

Note that even at this height the
pelvis has begun to tilt.

Fig. 12. X-RAY OF ABOVE

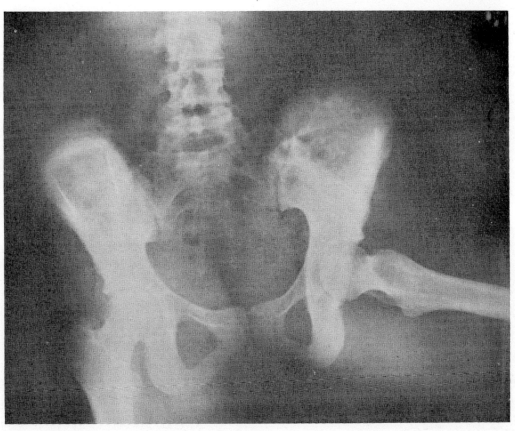

Fig. 13.
DÉVELOPPÉ À LA SECONDE
SHOWING PART PLAYED BY
SPINE AND PELVIS

Fig. 14.   X-RAY OF ABOVE

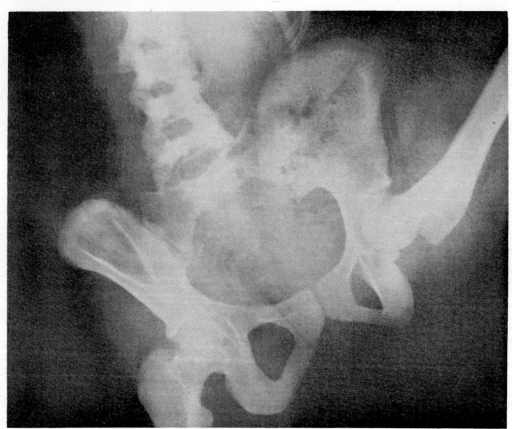

After this point, the pelvis and therefore the spine enter into the movement. Take, for example, *développé en avant*. The limit of hip flexion is reached at about the point shown in Fig. 10. Naturally training will increase this to a certain extent, but not so greatly as might be expected. Thereafter, the pelvis rolls on the supporting hip and the lumbar spine is straightened. In the beginner it is almost curved backward, as in sitting. In *développé à la seconde*, the pelvis is tilted sideways, the lumbar curve follows and the upper curves adjust. (Figs. 11–14.)

Similarly in arabesque, the extension of the hip, limited, by the way, by that important Y-shaped ligament in front, ceases at a certain point and thereafter the movement takes place in the spine. If the body is kept upright, the lumbar curve is greatly increased—dangerously so in its lower part where the strain is put upon the sacro-iliac and lumbo-sacral joints—but if the body leans slightly

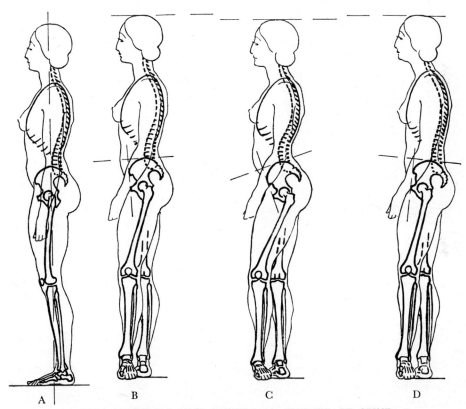

A   B   C   D

Fig. 15. NORMAL AND ABNORMAL CURVES OF SPINE

A. Correct position showing line of gravity of the body falling in front of ear, through pelvis and knee and in front of ankle joint.
B. Good position of pelvis in 5th position.
C. Pelvis tilted forward, hollow back and bent front knee.
D. Pelvis tilted back, lower back flattened.

Note that in ballet training the upper part of the back will become flattened (see text).

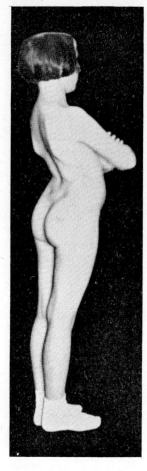

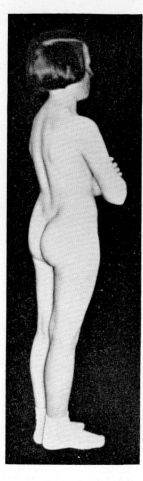

forward and the chest is lifted in the thoracic area, this spine is flattened to as great an extent as in a back bend.

These positions involve not so much movement, as adjustment, vertebra upon vertebra, and are immensely valuable in training both flexibility and posture, being performed by deep muscles connecting vertebra to vertebra, as well as by the long muscles on either side of the spine.

There is one other point to be mentioned in connection with the influence of the pelvis on the spine, and this concerns position rather than movement.

When the "tail" is "tucked in" the lumbar curve is straightened, and conversely when the "tail" sticks out the hollow is increased.* In the former position, because one curve influences another, the flattening of the lumbar spine is accompanied by a corresponding flattening

Fig. 16. AN 11-YEAR OLD SPINE WHICH PASSED FOR NORMAL IN BALLET DRESS AND WAS UNNOTICED IN TUNIC
(Cf. Fig. 15c)

Fig. 17. THE SAME AFTER SPECIAL CORRECTIVE EXERCISES, IMPROVED BUT NOT A NORMAL SPINE
(Cf. Fig. 15D)

of the other two curves, and the result is a spine which is practically without any normal forward and backward curves; in fact, a dead straight line. Aesthetically, this is pleasing, but the function of the curves is to absorb shock and therefore this type of back is vulnerable to strain and easily tired. Moreover, it is apt to lose in flexibility, especially in the lumbar region, making a high *arabesque* or *attitude* impossible.

The latter position, with the "tail sticking out", produces a hollow back and, at first, a corresponding rounding of the thoracic spine. As training proceeds,

* See Figs. 15C and D. In Fig. 15D the appearance is improved but the thoracic spine is still stiff and the gradual merging of thoracic into lumbar region is absent.

however, because of the special nature of ballet technique, the rounding of the thoracic spine is planed out and the hollow back continues higher, so that the lower ribs and chest are forced forward, producing an ugly torso, impairing breathing and putting great strain on the sacro-iliac joints.

This is the result in a very flexible back—one often found, for example, in acrobatically trained children. When, however, the back is less flexible, there may be found hard, resistant lower back muscles, which give rise to pain and prevent free movement.

The correct mid-way position for the holding of the pelvis is very important therefore, and on occasion a lesson with pupils in bathing dresses would be a help (and maybe a shock) to the teacher.

CHAPTER VI

THE KNEE JOINT

The lower end of the *femur* forms part of the knee joint, one of the most complicated joints of the body. In front it spreads into two *condyles* which merge into a smooth surface for articulation with the *patella*. Behind, the condyles form a deep depression, the *intercondyloid fossa*, which gives the familiar curved appearance to the back of the knee. On both outer and inner sides is a roughened projection or *epicondyle* which can be felt and often seen.

The upper end of the *tibia* articulates with the smooth under surface of the femur, so forming the knee joint. The hinge-like movement of the knee takes place between these two bones, but a small degree of rotation is also possible when the knee is bent. A note should be made of the position of the fibula on the outer side of the tibia. The head can be seen and felt just below and on the outer side of the knee.

The *patella* or knee-cap, although not strictly part of the knee joint, is attached to the tibia below by ligaments, and above receives the attachment of the powerful muscle on the front of the thigh, the quadratus femoris, which acts in completing the straightening of the joint, a movement with which every dancer is familiar.

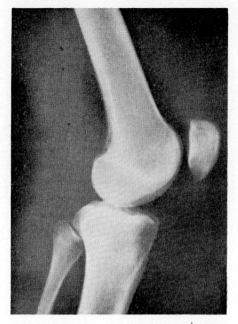
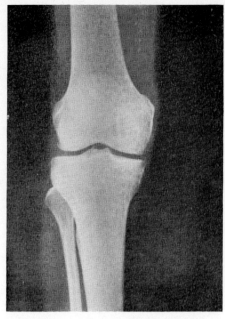

Fig. 18. (a) SIDE VIEW OF KNEE JOINT   (b) BACK VIEW OF KNEE JOINT
(BENT)   (STRAIGHT)

Friction between the bony surfaces of the patella and the femur is prevented by a large bursa, or sac of fluid, under the patella and a smaller bursa covers the front to protect against blows and pressure. (Too prolonged kneeling or continual crashing on to the knee after a leap may give rise to swelling of this bursa and exudation of fluid, causing stiffness and pain; in fact, "housemaid's knee". Inflammation of another bursa below the patella is a more serious condition.)

Lying on the flattened upper surface of the head of the tibia are the two semi-lunar cartilages, familiar source of trouble in the knee joint. The ligaments of the knee are complicated and can best be understood from the illustration.

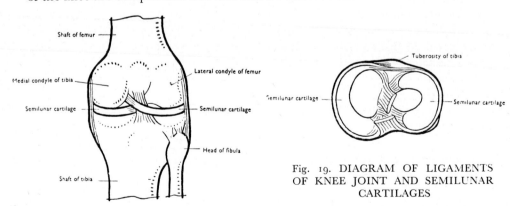

Fig. 19. DIAGRAM OF LIGAMENTS OF KNEE JOINT AND SEMILUNAR CARTILAGES

The ligaments secure the bones both vertically and crosswise and allow of a hinge-like movement in the knee joint, and, in addition, a small degree of rotation. During flexion and extension, i.e. the normal hinge-movement of the knee, the medial and lateral ligaments remain taut, but in a semi-flexed position (e.g. *fondu* or *demi-plié*) they relax and a small degree of side to side movement is possible. This position deprives the joint of the stabilisation of the ligaments (which, it will be remembered, safeguard joints against excessive range of movement). The medial ligament is attached to the medial cartilage and a transference of weight on to the inner side of the knee puts a strain upon that ligament. If the surrounding muscles are fully in control, the knee is able to sustain the strain, but a sudden twist in this position may cause too strong a pull; the ligament then drags on the cartilage which may be displaced in whole or in part. If this happens it can sometimes be replaced by manipulation but it is an accident which permanently weakens the joint and is liable to recur. So that movements which involve increasing the normal slight rotation of the knee joint (e.g. *ronds de jambe en l'air*) need counteracting by finishing each rotation with strong extension and straightening of the joint, whilst the performing of *ronds de jambe à terre* for example, with relaxed knee, is paving the way for later displacement of the internal cartilage.

A last and important point to remember about the knee joint is that, although its main action is similar to that of a hinge, a straightforward bending and straightening, at the last moment of straightening, a muscle on the inner side of the thigh comes into play and locks the joint with a slight rotation inwards. Similarly there is a tiny rotation outwards to unlock the joint. When the instruction is given to "pull up the thighs" the pupil is really being told to lock the knee joint and so give it its full stability and strength (and incidentally to produce an attractively smooth joint instead of a collection of knobs and bumps).

CHAPTER VII

THE FOOT

So far, the joints of the body which have been described are used in ballet much as in everyday life, but with a bigger range of movement. Their shape does not alter. With training the ligaments are stretched to obtain greater flexibility but the original shape of the joint is unchanged. With the foot, which is the next part of the body to consider, the situation is different. Dancing in any form makes considerable demands on the foot; in ballet, a unique demand. It has to become strong, very supple and as sensitive as the hand, and it is used in positions and movements quite outside its natural range. For this reason the original shape will be either an asset or a handicap but it will certainly not remain unchanged and therefore a detailed understanding of its structure is important.

The foot is composed of three parts, the *tarsus* consisting of seven tarsal bones corresponding to the carpal bones of the wrist; the five *metatarsals* corresponding to the carpal bones of the palm, and fourteen *phalanges* corresponding to the digits or fingers.

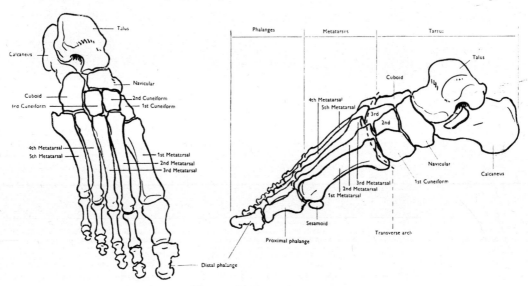

Fig. 20. DIAGRAM OF FOOT

The seven tarsal bones form the solid back part of the foot. They are separated from each other by protecting cartilage and bound firmly by ligaments which allow of a small degree of movement between the bones. The two largest of these bones are the *calcaneus* or heel bone, above which is the astragalus or *talus*. The weight of the body is taken first by the talus and transmitted through it to the calcaneus.

The heel, which can be seen and felt, is a projection of the calcaneus. On this projection and between it and the Achilles tendon is a protecting bursa. On the inner side of the calcaneus is a prominent lip, the *sustentaculum tali*, which provides support for the talus, the edge of which can often be seen or felt about one inch below the inner *malleolus* or ankle bone. On the outer side, in an almost corresponding position to the sustentaculum tali, is seen a projection of the calcaneus known as the *peroneal tubercle*.

In front of the calcaneus and articulating with it is the *cuboid*, not usually visible, but sometimes in dancers enlarged and prominent. It lies between the calcaneus and the two outer metatarsal bones and on the inner side articulates with the outer cuneiform and navicular or scaphoid. The *navicular* or scaphoid is on the inner side of the foot between the talus and cuneiform bones, articulating behind with the talus and in front with the three cuneiforms. On the inner side is a tuberosity which normally is not visible but which is clearly seen when the foot is "rolled". The three cuneiform bones articulate with each other and the inner three metacarpals in front, and with the navicular behind, whilst the outer also articulates with the cuboid.

Of the metatarsals and phalanges it need only be pointed out that the bony point seen about midway on the outer side of the foot belongs to the 5th (outer) metatarsal and that, as in the fingers, each toe has three phalanges whilst the big toe, like the thumb, has two.

Under the head of the first metatarsal, at the big toe joint are found two sesamoid bones, bones which do not enter into the formation of joints, but which act as a pulley for muscles to the big toe.

We have mentioned several bony points which can be seen. Study your own foot and identify them:

Inner and outer (medial and lateral) malleoli or ankle bones.
Back of calcaneus—heel.
Sustentaculum tali.
Peroneal tubercle.
Tuberosity of navicular.
Head of 5th metatarsal.

The arrangement of the bones of the foot is such that two arches are formed; one the longitudinal along the inner side formed by the calcaneus, talus, navicular, the three cuneiforms and the first three metatarsal; and the other transversely across the forefoot.

Normally these arches have a good deal of elasticity, but may give if subjected to too great a strain. The talus sustains the weight of the body, transmitted to it through the tibia, and it is therefore being constantly pushed downwards. Should it not be able to resist this pressure the talus and the

3

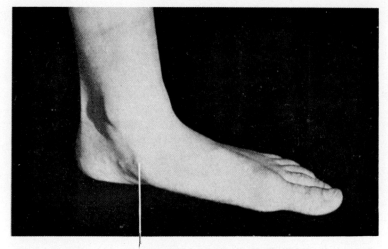

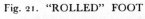

Tuberosity of navicular in "rolled" foot

Fig. 21. "ROLLED" FOOT

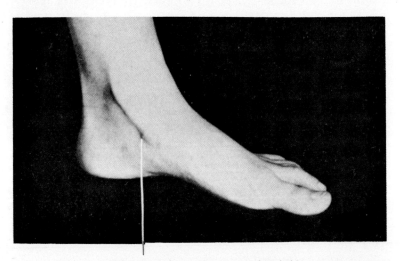

Tuberosity of navicular in same foot held in correct position

Fig. 22. NORMAL FOOT POSITION

navicular may be forced out of position. The head of the navicular can then clearly be seen, often almost touching the ground. (See Figs. 21 and 22.) (In ballet, the prime cause of this collapse is rolling and it can be understood, therefore, how important it is to prevent this from the earliest beginnings.)

The transverse arch is formed by the convex arrangement of the tarsal and metatarsal bones across the forefoot. Should this structure give way, the heads of the metatarsals may sink even to floor level and give rise to much pain from

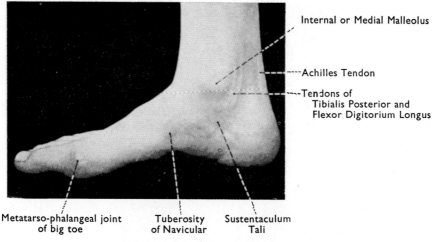

Internal or Medial Malleolus

Achilles Tendon

Tendons of
Tibialis Posterior and
Flexor Digitorium Longus

Metatarso-phalangeal joint   Tuberosity   Sustentaculum
of big toe   of Navicular   Tali

Fig. 23. SURFACE MARKINGS OF FOOT

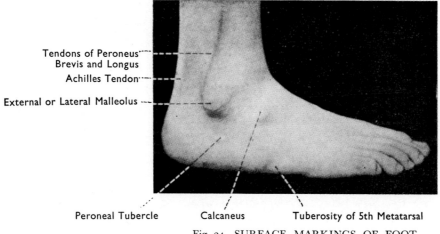

Tendons of Peroneus
Brevis and Longus

Achilles Tendon

External or Lateral Malleolus

Peroneal Tubercle   Calcaneus   Tuberosity of 5th Metatarsal

Fig. 24. SURFACE MARKINGS OF FOOT

resulting strain on ligaments, muscles and nerves; but it is rare to find this sinking of the transverse arch without the beginnings at least of flattening of the longitudinal arch.

This describes sufficiently for our purpose the bare bones of the foot. They should be learnt by drawing, again and yet again, so that what follows will seem simple and logical instead of confusing and difficult. If the eye has a clear picture of the position and shape of the bones, ligaments and muscles may be slipped into place and the action of the foot understood without more than an occasional tear!

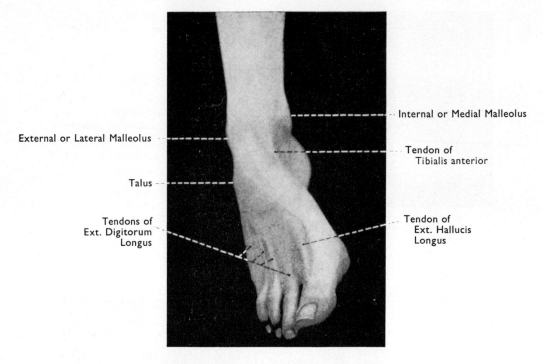

Internal or Medial Malleolus

External or Lateral Malleolus

Tendon of
Tibialis anterior

Talus

Tendons of
Ext. Digitorum
Longus

Tendon of
Ext. Hallucis
Longus

Fig. 25. SURFACE MARKINGS OF FOOT

CHAPTER VIII

LIGAMENTS OF FOOT AND ANKLE JOINT

We have already said that the bones of the tarsus and the forefoot are bound to each other by short ligaments. These hold the bones firmly together but are not entirely responsible for the arches of the foot. The arches are formed first by the architectural arrangement of the bones but are held together in the second place by these short and other important long ligaments, and maintained finally by muscles.

The chief long ligaments concerned are:

Spring ligament.
Long plantar or sole ligament.
Short plantar or sole ligament.

The spring ligament is the most important ligament of the foot. It is attached to the sustentaculum tali and to the plantar or sole surface of the navicular, so that it supports that important ankle bone, the talus.

Under the foot are the long and short plantar ligaments, the long attached at one end to the under surface of the calcaneus and the other to the three middle metatarsals.

The short plantar ligament lies under the long, and is attached at one end to the calcaneus and passes forward and a little outward to the cuboid.

Two other ligaments should be noted, those which are concerned in the ankle joint itself. On the inner side is the medial or deltoid ligament attached above to the end of the tibia and spreading below into three bands attached to the tuberosity of the navicular, the sustentaculum tali and the body of the talus.

On the outer side is the lateral ligament attached above to the end of the fibula and also dividing into three bands, one to the front of the talus, one passing downwards to the calcaneus and the third horizontally backward to the body of the talus. Rupture of any of the fibres of this ligament is familiar to the victim of a "sprained ankle".

Ligaments are important structures. As we have already learnt, they bind bones together, thus forming a joint; they can be stretched, but if unduly, cannot then return to their original length. Finally, they guard the joint, preventing dislocation and abnormal movement.

A generation ago it was held that the ligaments of the foot supported the arch and that the stretching of these ligaments was the cause of the dropping of the arch. Today it is considered by most authorities (though not without some controversy) that the function of the ligaments is to bind the bones together and hold them in position during standing and movement, whilst it is the muscles of the foot and leg which maintain the arch, and failure in the strength and tone of these muscles will result in the changed position of the bones, causing stretching of the ligaments and the resulting fallen arches.

As far as ballet is concerned, it is as well to bear both possibilities in mind, especially in dealing with young children. Ligaments are easily stretched in the young. Ballet technique is designed to stretch them in order, as we have said, that the foot may become completely flexible. In the *correctly trained foot* the muscles are completely able to control the situation. There is no rolling of the talus inward. The foot merely assumes, to a greater or lesser extent, varying according to its type, a plane position in which the arch is not visible when standing but as soon as movement is required the muscles are in action and the arch forms.* This is a completely different picture from "flat foot" in which the relative positions of the bones have changed and the muscles are unable to function correctly.

On the other hand, the real "flat foot" can easily be produced by early imperfect training, and so it is worth while to get a more detailed understanding of the mechanism of the foot and ankle joint.

* *The foot which maintains the arch in standing is more frequently found in dancers today than formerly. (See Frontispiece.)*

CHAPTER IX

MOVEMENTS OF THE FOOT AND ANKLE JOINT

Some functional similarity may be found between the movements of the foot and those of the spine. In the latter we found that there are two functions, that of adjusting for weight bearing, in order to maintain the upright position (as in développés for example), and that of definite movement as in side-bending, etc. So it is with the foot. Sometimes it functions as a weight-bearing apparatus and sometimes it is used for propulsion or other movements. In the spine the adjustment function was performed largely by the long muscles of the back, reinforced by small muscles passing from vertebra to vertebra. In the foot there is a similar though not identical arrangement, in which four layers of short muscles along the sole of the foot adjust the bones of the foot to the shape required and hold them in this position, whilst the long muscles attached to these bones and travelling up the leg are used in the performance of the various movements.

It will simplify the description of these movements if we refer to them by their anatomical names:

Pointing the foot downward is known as *plantar flexion*, and the reverse, turning up, as *dorsi-flexion*.

The inner border can be raised by *inversion*, the outer by *eversion*.

The forefoot may be turned in, *adduction;* or out, *abduction*.

The combined action of adduction and inversion is known as *supination*, and of abduction and eversion as *pronation*.

Plantar and dorsi-flexion take place in the ankle joint itself. They are limited partly by the shape of the bones and tightness of surrounding ligaments and, in dorsi-flexion, by the length of the Achilles tendon, that strong familiar tendon of the calf muscle inserted on the back of the calcaneus. (Plantar flexion is often accompanied in children by supination, or, in the language of the studio "sickling-in" of the foot. This is normal, as it is Nature's method of developing the arch.)

Inversion in which the inner border of the foot is raised, and the opposite, *eversion*, in which the outer border is lifted, take place in the back part of the foot, between the articulating surfaces of the talus and calcaneus. Inversion, as we have just said, is the position of "sickling-in" (when combined with plantar flexion), eversion corresponds to "sickling-out". When the foot is used in standing, however, it is by eversion combined with abduction that the foot is "rolled" (so that the reverse, inversion with adduction, is the correction, taking place in the mid-tarsal and back part of the foot whilst the heel, *ball of big toe* and outer border of the foot hold the ground).

Ad- and *abduction*, in which the *forefoot* turns in or out, take place in the mid-tarsal region, i.e. between the talus, navicular, calcaneus and cuboid bones.

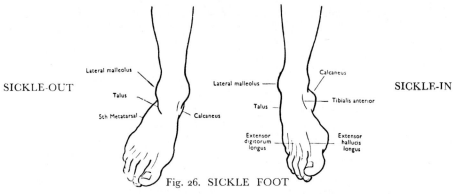

Fig. 26. SICKLE FOOT

This turning in and out of the *forefoot* must not be confused with the *turning of the whole foot*, which is that used in ballet, *and which takes place in the hip joint*.

The toes are important in stabilising the foot when weight-bearing. They also have two movements—flexion or curling downward, and the reverse of this, extension; whilst in some people there is a remnant of the once free movement of the big toe outward and inward. These movements are practically independent of ankle and foot movements, but there is an almost natural tendency to flex the toes in the effort to increase the degree of plantar flexion, for which the reason will be given later.

Muscle Action of Foot

The muscle action of the leg and foot is never easy to understand and under the conditions in which it is used in ballet it is doubly complicated. Nevertheless, because it is of such great importance, we will try to give as simple a picture of it as possible.

The foot is used in five capacities:

1. Weight-bearing.
2. Propulsion.
3. Shock-absorbing.
4. Lifting the body as in springing and *relevé* movements.
5. Free movement without weight bearing (as in *battements frappés*, etc).

All these movements are performed by a series of muscles attached, with one exception, below the knee at one end and to various bones of the foot at the other; and by the four layers of short muscles on the sole of the foot. The one exception is that of the *gastrocnemius*, the big calf muscle which arises above the knee and ends in the Achilles tendon. This muscle, therefore, acts both on the knee joint (bending) and on the ankle joint, lifting the heel when the foot is on the ground, pointing the foot when this is in the air. Apart from this, the leg muscles may be divided into two groups, those which are situated on the outer side of the front of the leg and pass round the outer ankle or over the front of the ankle. These dorsiflex the foot. The second set pass down the inner side and round the inner ankle and plantar flex.

Unfortunately for our peace of mind, each of these muscles has at least two actions. They will be more easily understood if they are tabulated and learnt in conjunction with Figs. 23–27.

Name	Action
Tibialis anterior	Dorsiflexes and inverts the foot
Extensor hallucis longus	Dorsiflexes the foot. Extends big toe
Extensor digitorum longus	Dorsiflexes and everts the foot. Also extends outer four toes
Peroneus tertius	Dorsiflexes and everts the foot

These are the muscles which turn the foot up and which also raise the inner or outer border. The long extensor hallucis turn up the big toe and the long extensor digitorum, ending in four slips, the remaining four toes. Tibialis anterior is an extremely important muscle since it is attached to the inner cuneiform bone and first metatarsal and therefore helps to maintain the arch of the foot.

The second group of muscles, those which point or plantar flex, are:

Name	Action
Peroneus longus	Plantar flexes and everts the foot
Peroneus brevis	Plantar flexes and everts the foot
Tibialis posterior	Plantar flexes and inverts the foot
Flexor digitorum longus	Plantar flexes foot and flexes the four outer toes, and is also connected with short muscles of the sole
Flexor hallucis longus	Holds the big toe to the ground and is sometimes described as the "taking off" muscle. When the foot is in the air it flexes big toe

In this group two muscles are of special interest. Tibialis posterior passes round the inner ankle and then under the navicular and inner cuneiform bones, where it is inserted on their under surfaces. In addition, it sends out slips to the under surface of several bones of the foot and is therefore an important supporter of the arch. (It is in the tendon of this muscle, as it passes round the inner ankle, that pain is sometimes felt in *pointe* work, and where occasionally is found a synovitis, i.e. inflammation in the synovial membrane surrounding the tendon.)

The other muscle to note is flexor hallucis longus, often described as the bowspring of the arch. In springing or propulsion it momentarily fixes the big toe to the ground and then assists in the take-off. This muscle, and the tibialis posterior and tibialis anterior, are the most important of the long muscles in assisting the sole muscles to maintain the arch. They are also the most important muscles in maintaining the normal relation between the front and back part of the foot, that part composed of the irregular tarsal bones, and the forefoot,

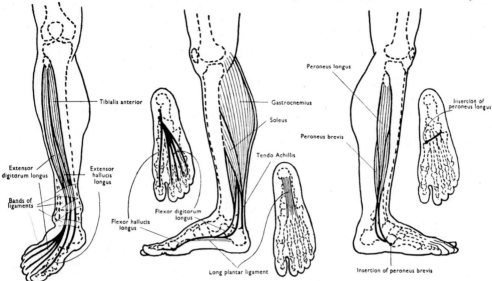

Fig. 27. MUSCLES OF LEG AND FOOT

beginning with the long metatarsals—the region where the small movements of inversion and adduction take place, and their reverse, eversion and abduction. Note also the double action of flexor digitorum longus, which accounts for the tendency to curl the toes when pointing the foot. The two actions can however be separated.

Before leaving the muscle action of the foot, there are one or two points to be noticed about the small muscles of the sole. These we know to be concerned chiefly with the changing shape of the foot—compact or spread, long or short. They propel the foot in springing and walking and hold the toes firmly on the ground in standing, preventing splaying and holding up the arch. They are immensely important but may be considered as a whole. In one only is there any separate movement, the *abductor hallucis* which, in young children and an occasional adult, still has the remnant of power to separate the big toe from its neighbours, as the thumb is separate from the fingers. In most human beings, however, its power has been lost in the adaptive changes of evolution; to this loss of power is due the ease with which the big toe is deflected, with subsequent enlargement of the joint and the resulting *Hallux valgus* or bunion. What spreading of the toes remains is by the action of the long muscles and can only be performed in combination with extension, i.e. turning up of the toes, not as a pure movement.

The important business now remains of recognising the muscles of the foot, when they are sufficiently near the surface to be seen. Therefore study the illustrations and compare them with your own foot. Never mind that you cannot remember their names, just know of their existence and position. Names are not necessary to teach dancing but appreciation of the shape of the normal foot and its muscles is a helpful guide to the watchful eye.

CHAPTER X

THE FOOT IN ORDER AND DISORDER

It can be taken as axiomatic that *the foot which functions correctly when it is weight-bearing will function correctly in movement.* This is a point which is apt to be neglected by teachers, the concentration being rather upon the action of the feet in dancing alone. But it is at the barre, in standing, on one or both feet, that very important training is being given.

In standing, i.e. when the foot is taking the weight of the body, it should be holding the ground at three points: behind, the back of the calcaneus; in front the heads of the 1st and 5th metatarsals. This triangle constitutes a base from which the muscles of the leg and sole of the foot can work strongly in holding up the arch. In this position the long muscles of the leg, those previously discussed, having no actual movements to perform, give the ankle and foot the stability necessary for balance. If the supporting foot is observed, for example, during barre exercises, the tendons of tibialis anterior and extensor digitorum longus can easily be seen over the front of the ankle, coming and going, whilst the twitchings on the outer side of the leg betray the activity of the muscles themselves.

In order that these muscles and the deeper ones, which cannot be seen, should function at their best, the foot must hold the ground on the triangular base, and the leg must be kept in a vertical position over the foot and at its natural angle, i.e. *when the foot is approximately at a right angle to the leg, and the forefoot is in alignment with the back of the foot.* This becomes increasingly difficult as the foot is "turned" more and more. Whilst in the early stages the turning takes place entirely in the hip joint, this alignment is not disturbed. There comes a moment, however, as training progresses, when a still further degree of turning is required, and then the leg muscles must work very strongly to prevent abduction of the forefoot. These muscles, we found earlier, are the inverters, tibialis anterior and posterior, in particular. Should this final turning be mechanically impossible to the individual pupil, should it be insisted upon too early, the evertors will win the day and not only will the foot "roll" with subsequent weakening of the whole musculature of the foot, but an ugly bulge of muscle will be developed on the outer side of the leg, giving evidence to their superior strength. The importance, therefore, of turning the foot only in so far as the balance of these muscles can be maintained cannot be over-estimated.

The short sole muscles are well catered for in ballet technique. Their work is not spectacular but very important. They hold the foot in the shape required and it is in such movements as *battements tendus* and *frappés* that they are mostly developed, since in them the foot as a whole is narrowed and shortened. But there is at best only very weak work in the sole muscles of the foot unless they are stimulated by contact with the floor. Not passing over any large joint, they have no power of shortening and lengthening as the joint is moved; they function merely by shortening in their own length as the foot changes in shape. When, however, there is pressure on the floor, as in standing, or stimulation by pressure on the floor as the foot passes into another position, they come into full play, and it can therefore be understood why the striking and pushing downwards on the floor is important in these special exercises. If blocked shoes are worn exclusively in early training, part of this work is inhibited, since the stiff sole holds the foot in the required shape instead of the muscles, which are then supported, so that movement takes place almost entirely in the ankle joint and is, as we now know, then performed by the long leg muscles. This will produce the appearance of a high arch but will not give the dancer the required strength and sensitiveness of foot necessary for her work.

The foot of one individual varies as much from his neighbour's as does his hand, or even his face. There is hardly such a thing as a "normal" foot. What makes it normal is its capacity to meet the demands made upon it, and in ballet these are very great. A very highly arched foot will not take as kindly to hard work as a sturdier foot, more closely knit, such as is seen in Fig. 28A. This type will stand up to wear and tear and give no trouble. On the other hand, the foot in Fig. 28B has an arch beginning practically in the ankle joint itself, leaving the forefoot soft and flexible, and will always be beautiful rather than very strong. Fig. 28C has a high arch formed by the mid-tarsal joints with a less flexible ankle joint, a stronger foot and still beautiful. Since, however, beauty as well as strength is the coveted possession of every dancer, the one must be safeguarded whilst the other is being cultivated. The safeguarding begins with the first lesson. The guiding principle of the teacher should be that the foot must hold the ground, big toe, little toe, heel, and the *alignment of the foot to the leg and thigh must never be altered*. But it must always be remembered that the foot has no independent existence. It begins with the head, back, pelvis, and finishes with the thigh and leg. In so far as the back is flexible, the pelvis in its right relation to the spine, the hip joints sufficiently flexible, so far can the leg be turned and a safe 5th position taken. Neglect of this most elementary precept is the source of the painful foot, the enlarged big toe joint, and even back strain, which have forced many a promising student to abandon her career. The good teacher recognises instinctively this interdependence of one part of the body to the other. It takes us farther afield into the borderland between anatomy and physiology, and so we will follow it up in as simple a form as possible in considering posture and "placing".

A B C

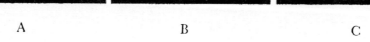

A B C

A   B   C

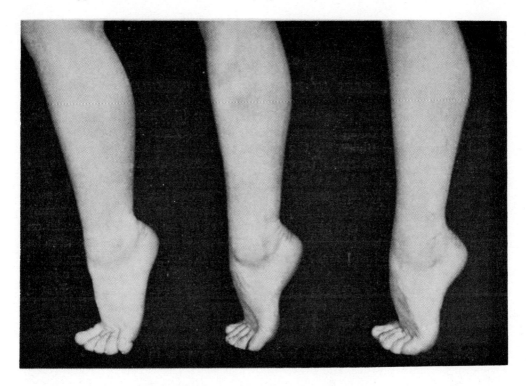

Fig. 28. THREE TYPES OF FOOT

A. Strongly knit with little arch.
B. High arch beginning in ankle joint with long forefoot.
C. High arch in which tarsal bones are more prominent and arch appears in forefoot.

CHAPTER XI

MUSCLES IN POSTURE AND "PLACING"

Muscles in movement have three characteristics: (i) They can contract, i.e. shorten, and in so doing become bulkier. (ii) They can extend or lengthen. (iii) They have elasticity, i.e. the power of returning to their original length after contraction or extension (as opposed to ligaments which, it will be remembered, can be stretched, but if unduly will not then return to their original length). The simplest and most familiar example of shortening and lengthening can be seen in the action of biceps and triceps muscles. When the elbow is deliberately bent, biceps contracts and gets bulkier, whilst at the same time the muscles on the back of the arm lengthen. When the arm is straightened the muscles return to their original length. That, however, is merely an illustration and is an over-simplified picture, for no one muscle produces a movement of a joint. In any movement of everyday life (or of dancing) an extremely complicated mechanism is brought into action, involving many muscle groups. The study of such mechanisms is beyond the scope of this book and not necessary for the teacher of ballet. There is, however, a further characteristic of living muscles which concerns her and which is of vital importance in the maintenance of body posture, and that is known as *muscle tone*. This is a state which has nothing to do with bulk or strength, but is a device of the central nervous system to keep the muscle in a state of preparedness for movement. In health, tone is good; in fatigue or debility, it is poor. Tone can be improved by exercise but it is largely dependent on the health of the body in general and the state of the nervous system in particular. It is produced by a series of stimulations from the brain to the spinal cord and thence to the muscles. It cannot be produced by any act of will, nor by conscious, controlled movement and is therefore known as "reflex".

It is this reflex stimulation which keeps the muscles at the required length. A simple example is found in the muscles of the jaw by which the mouth is kept closed. This does not require an effort of muscular contraction. Nor do the muscles tire. They remain at the required length so long as the reflex is in operation. When, as sometimes happens in sleep, this reflex ceases to operate, the muscles lengthen and the jaw drops. Again, an infant's head drops forward until, by repeated efforts, it is able to hold it in the normal position. This is not due to the strengthening of the neck muscles alone, but also to the establishing of the reflex control from the brain. If this reflex cannot be established—as in certain defects of the brain—the child's head will loll, and it will not be able to hold it in the required position. No exercises will remedy this, because the lack is not in the strength of the muscles but in their connection with the brain.

46

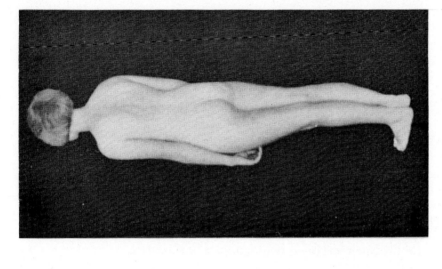

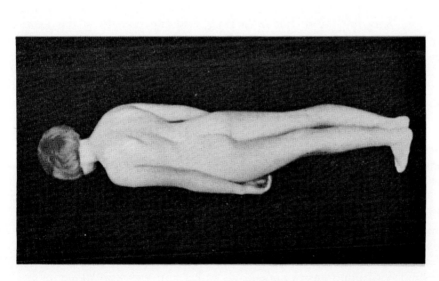

Fig. 29. BAD POSTURE—BEFORE AND AFTER TREATMENT

Typical bad posture due solely to loss of muscle tone.

The same after treatment which included ballet technique combined with adequate rest, an important and often neglected factor in cases of this type.

So it is with all those muscles upon which the upright posture of the body depends. They take up a given length and are held in this length by this reflex control arising in the brain and generated by the nerves of the spinal cord. No one group works independently of others; changes in one affect the whole system of control. Thus, should certain of the muscles of the spine, through habit or wrong training, be functioning at an incorrect length, asymmetry or other defects of posture will be found in the spine and possibly throughout the whole body, even being noticeable in the knees and feet. Useless to try to correct this by active movements since it is the reflex control, not strength, which is at fault. This control can be restored, not by movement, but, in the words of a prominent orthopaedic surgeon, by *absence* of movement, i.e. by the muscles being held at the required length, in the required position, whilst the rest of the body is performing other movements, until this required length becomes automatic, i.e. controlled by the reflex mechanism derived from the brain.

Reflex control, not muscular effort, is the key to the upright position of the body; not, for example, the pulling back of the shoulders and throwing out of the chest by sustained effort and contraction of shoulder and spinal muscles, but a lengthening of the spine by adjustment, a sensing of the body which is effortless and by which no fatigue is produced in the muscles.

This is a picture which the ballet dancer will recognise, for it is that of the fundamental position at the barre. If this is taken correctly, the important lower leg and foot muscles are balancing each other so that the foot is held in the correct position; the knees are locked, the hip muscles shortened to hold the pelvis in a firm position and from this stable foundation the spine can be lengthened without muscular effort, but by sensing, and can be held in this length for long periods, whilst the head is freely movable without tension in the neck muscles. Every time this position is repeated—hundreds of times, maybe, in the course of a lesson—the reflexes controlling the required posture are being educated, or in the words of the ballet teacher, the body is becoming "placed". *The pupil who lacks this placing lacks it because her initial position at the barre has been faulty and the required reflexes have not been established.* One further note:

Our sense of our position in space, which includes our recognition and knowledge of how we are standing, kneeling, etc., is dependent on a very complex mechanism. The latter includes visual stimuli and use of the muscles controlling the movements of the eyeball, a balance organ in the inner ear, and unconscious impressions reaching the nervous system from muscles, tendons, joints, etc., but especially from the soles of the feet. These are stimulated by contact with the ground; those in the eyes by the act of focussing; and those in the inner ear cannot be controlled, but work in conjunction with the eyes. Thus, a child born blind has to depend upon feet and inner ear alone for her sense of the upright position, and therefore has great difficulty in acquiring a normal head position and a normal gait. A child who loses its sight even as early as two years does not have the same difficulty because the reflexes have once been established and leave a memory in the muscles. Again, standing on the top of a high cliff, looking out into space, many people lose their sense of balance and tend to sway. If the eyes are focussed on some fixed point, balance is gradually restored. Similarly, if the inner ear reflexes are disturbed by spinning of the body, giddiness results. If the eyes are focussed on some fixed point, the giddiness is quickly overcome. And if, as in performing *petits tours* and *pirouettes*, the eyes are focussed on a fixed point for the split second on each turn, the beginner who falls about on the first lesson quickly learns to turn innumerable times without giddiness and loss of balance. In the words of anatomy, her ocular and vestibular reflexes have become highly trained.

This interdependence of posture, balance and highly co-ordinated movement is developed to perfection in ballet training. Remembering, however, that it begins with the starting position of every exercise at the barre, the teacher of ballet should forget the language of anatomy and use her own—"Don't roll your feet, straighten your knees, pull up your thighs, lift up from your hips, stretch your ribs, lengthen your back, lower your shoulders, loosen your neck"—and lastly, the somewhat neglected "raise your eyes, look outward".

4

CHAPTER XII

COMMON FAULTS

In this chapter an attempt will be made to show the origin of the faults commonly met with at the barre. The exercises themselves are not described since details of execution belong to a text-book on dancing, but an exception is made in the case of *pliés* and *développés*, for faults in these important exercises show themselves in practically everything that follows.

Pliés in 1st, 3rd and 5th positions

In these three positions practically the same faults occur. For clarity the movement may be divided into four parts:

1. The knees are bent out with the whole foot firmly on the floor and the knees pressed outward as far as possible.
2. The heels are raised in order to allow of still further bending outward of the knees. This raising should be as little as possible.
3. The knees are *pressed outward* and slightly straightened as the heels are pressed downward to the floor.
4. The knees are straightened and starting position resumed. Throughout the spine is held upright.

Now let us consider the common faults and their anatomical results:

1. Remembering the importance of the training of posture by "absence of movement" if the starting and finishing positions are inaccurate, the body will habitually adopt those positions after a certain number of repetitions. The most common fault of starting and finishing is hollowing of the back. This is mainly because of the pull of the Y-shaped ligament of the hips which prevents the outward rotation of the hips. The pelvis then tilts forward, with corresponding change in the lumbar curve. Therefore the feet must be turned only so far as this ligament allows in the hip joint until, by training, it has been sufficiently stretched, when the back can be held in its correct position if the hips and feet are fully turned.
2. As the knees bend outward the heels want to lift. The chief reason for this is the pull of the Achilles tendon. This strong tendon can only be lengthened, if at all, in very young children, but except in rare cases, its length in relation to the leg and foot muscles is arranged for by nature to give the best mechanical working of the leg and foot, and therefore there is the moment, varying in each individual, when the pull is felt and the heel should rise in the downward movement of the *plié*.
3. "Sitting" at the end of the downward movement. This takes place in the hip joints. The result is that the back and abdominal muscles relax and,

in effect, it is the same as if the spine were bent forward and the knees drawn up to the chest, completely destroying the value of the *plié*.

4. Both on the downward and upward movement a *most* common fault is the rolling of the feet. It is an axiom that must never be forgotten and cannot be repeated too often, that the *relation of the foot to the leg must never alter*. In other words, the weight of the body must be received by the talus, transmitted to the calcaneus and distributed in the mid region and strongest part of the foot. When the feet are rolled, this relationship of foot to leg is disturbed. The weight falls on the inner side of the foot, largely on the big toe joint. The muscle imbalance causes overaction of the evertors and above all, undue splaying of the forefoot whereby the subsequent enlarging and outward displacement of the big toe joint is made easy. This common disability of the dancer, often ascribed solely to *pointe* work, begins with the rolling foot in *pliés*. Therefore the complete turning of the foot should be delayed until, by many months or even years of training, the relative position of foot to leg can be maintained throughout the exercise, and the foot can hold the ground on its three points of contact.

5. On the upward movement, the knees tend to fall inward. This is because of the action of the muscles which normally push the body upwards when the knees are bent. These are muscles on the inner side of the thigh and back of the hip; using them, it is relatively easy to straighten the knees, but in doing so the feet will roll and this, at all costs, must be avoided. Therefore the knees must be pressed outward so that the leg and foot retain their correct alignment, and in so doing the postural muscles of the back will automatically play their very important part—an action which is lost if the knees fall inward.

6. Failure to straighten the knees completely when finishing. Mechanically this is difficult, especially in 3rd and 5th positions. Yet, if we remember its anatomy, the slightly bent knee is an enemy of the dancer. Sometimes this fault is encouraged, if not acquired, by an insufficient pause between one movement and the next.

Pliés in 2nd position

In the 2nd position the chief faults, other than those already dealt with, are the lifting of the heels, and a common tendency to "sit" or bend forward in the waist, both due to tightness of the Y-shaped ligament and inner muscles of the thigh. "Rolling" is more easy to detect in this position, and is corrected by the pressing outwards of the knees.

Pliés in 4th position

The special difficulty in this position is to avoid twisting the hips. Perhaps more than in any *plié*, the effort to keep the pelvis square and the body "placed" strengthens the postural muscles of the spine.

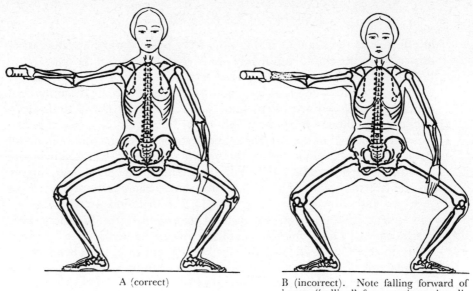

A (correct)

B (incorrect). Note falling forward of knees, "rolling" feet, sagging spine diminishing chest cavity with interference with breathing and loss of height.

Fig. 30. PLIÉS À LA SECONDE

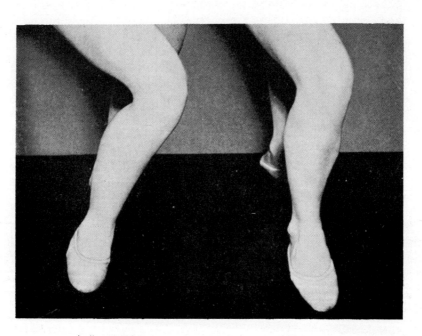

A (incorrect)   B (correct)

Side view of pliés à la seconde. Note effect on foot of falling forward of knees in A.

Fig. 31. PLIÉS À LA SECONDE

We are dealing here with anatomy and not with system and so the question of ports-de-bras during *pliés*—if any and of what kind—is a question rather for the teacher than the anatomist. We can, however, observe that whatever arm movements are used, the attention of the teacher must first and foremost be drawn to the correct execution of the movement itself and not distracted from it either by arm or head movements, even though they form an integral part of the whole.

One final word on the subject of *pliés*. We have stressed the word pressure in our analysis—pressure outward of the knees and downward on the floor. The reason for the former is obvious: to maintain the correct alignment of foot to leg, with the secondary result of the stretching of the inner thigh muscles and so increasing the flexibility of the hips. Just as important is the pressure downward with the whole foot on the floor. This distinguishes *pliés* from the ordinary heel-raising and knee-bending of other systems. Its value is in supplying resistance to the foot, leg and hip muscles, thus increasing their strength, whilst the holding of the back by the non-muscular sensing of its length is the foundation of that good posture which is characteristic of the ballet dancer.

Battements Tendus

This is a movement which should take place in the hip joint, ankle and forefoot only. The most common fault perhaps is the slackening of the knee and the reason is to be found on the supporting side. In normal life, when standing on one leg, the pelvis tilts upwards to the side of the supporting leg and the hip joint is carried a little outward, away from the mid-line of the body. But the dancer's whole effort is to keep the body always in the mid-line whatever it is doing. That is the secret of "placing", and so a strong muscular effort of the hip muscles is required to keep this alignment. This in turn calls into action the back and abdominal muscles of the supporting side. The external resistance offered by the barre aids this effort. Every dancer knows the added difficulty of making it when in the centre. When, however, the beginner attempts this adjustment, it frequently happens that the muscles are not sufficiently strong to maintain it. Without it, there is not enough clearance from the ground for the working leg and so the knee bends in order to shorten the leg. This is especially the case on the inward movement. A bent knee is a weak knee. It is also an ugly knee.

There may be another reason for the yielding but, as it will operate more noticeably in grands battements and développés, we will return to it later.

The second fault commonly found is the avoiding of the last bit of effort needed to slide the foot in with the heel absolutely down in the closing into the 5th or 3rd positions. It is a question of attention rather than any special anatomical reason, unless by chance the Achilles tendon is tight or short, when special and continued practice is necessary.

There will of course always be the effort needed to keep the leg out-turned, but in all exercises taken on one foot, a special difficulty arises which will be

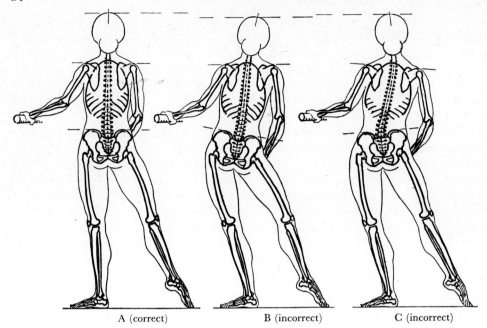

A (correct)   B (incorrect)   C (incorrect)

Fig. 32. DÉGAGÉ À LA SECONDE
Note tilt of pelvis, shoulders and head in B and C.

discussed here, but which should be borne in mind in all subsequent movements. It is the prevention of the rolling of the *supporting* foot. This rolling is due to the tendency of the pelvis to twist towards the working leg and so to avoid the pull on the Y-shaped ligament and the inner thigh muscles on the supporting side, especially when the movement is being performed in 2nd position. (In fact, this twisting can be taken so far that the movement becomes almost 4th position.) If this happens, the forefoot remains the fixed point upon which the femur and tibia fall inwards. The tibia carries with it the talus, and the result is the familiar roll. If the degree is greater than can be corrected by muscular effort the foot should not be turned so far, or the result will be a weakened foot and an ugly bulge on the outside of the leg due to the overaction of the evertors of the foot.

Sickling out in *battement tendus derrière* is an especially bad fault since the pressure on the inner side of the forefoot displaces momentarily the big toe joint. When this is repeated many times in each lesson it is easy to see it may be the beginning of an enlargement of the joint (see Fig. 33).

A last fault in battements tendus is the clenching of the toes, which partly takes the place of the action of the muscles in the sole. (See pp. 40–41. Action of Flex. Dig. Longus.) Associated with this is found a tendency to avoid the strong push on the floor, beginning with the whole foot in the outward movement, thus losing the strength which results from working against resistance.

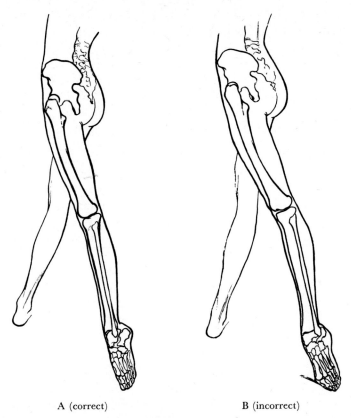

A (correct)   B (incorrect)

Fig. 33. DÉGAGÉ DERRIÈRE

B the foot is sickled-out, pressure falling on the side of the big toe, displacing that and other toes.

Grands Battements

The correct performance of grands battements includes battements tendus, and in that part of the movement the same faults are likely to appear. In the lift or throw of the leg, however, there is more difficulty in maintaining a vertical position of the body, neither leaning over the barre nor swinging away from it. This is mainly a question of the beginning and finish, which if correct, establishes and strengthens by repetition the holding of the back.

In *grands battements en avant*, there may be difficulty in keeping the working knee straight, due to the pull of the hamstring muscles at the back of the thigh. Nevertheless, this is one of the best exercises for lengthening them, so that practice should overcome the trouble. The same shortening will cause the supporting knee to bend. It is better by far to keep the movement lower, and with the supporting knee straight, than to continue to practise with it yielding, since the hamstrings of the working leg then lose the fixed point from which to stretch.

Anatomically, the strain on the lumbar spine is very great if grands battements *en arrière* are taken from the completely upright position. It will be remembered that extension of the hip is soon transferred to the spine (see Chap. V). If this is prevented, certainly the range of movement will be increased, but at some risk of injury to the relatively soft intervertebral discs. The strain on the sacro-iliac joint is also increased and, moreover, the rigid holding of the spine necessary to isolate the movement to the hip joint deprives it of a very valuable opportunity for increasing its flexibility. On the other hand, it is possible, by leaning forward too far, to perform the movement almost entirely in the upper lumbar region, when the hip joint moves to its minimum instead of maximum extension.

Grands battements à la seconde demand, as in battements tendus, strong holding on the supporting side to prevent an actual bending of the spine to that side. Some degree is inevitable since, as the leg rises, there is a sideways tilt of the pelvis (see Figs. 12–14) but it should be kept as controlled as possible and no telescoping of the ribs allowed.

Grands battements en arrière are difficult because of the limited range of extension in the hip joint. The greater part of the movement takes place in the lumbar spine and great flexibility in this region is needed.

Ronds de Jambe à terre

The difficulty in *ronds de jambe à terre* is to find sufficient clearance from the ground for the moving leg, and the remedy is the correct alignment of the body over the supporting leg (see Fig. 32). If this is incorrect and the body is allowed to sag towards the barre, the knee of the working leg will perforce bend as the movement passes from 4th behind, through 1st position. The result of continuous practice with a slightly bent knee will be a stretching of the inner or medial ligament of the knee and a weakening of its support. Invariably this is accompanied by a "rolling" foot and, because of the resistance of the floor and the strength which is used on the inner border of the foot in this very incorrect position, all the evils of "rolling" are increased. In young children especially, where the structures involved are pliable, a close watch should be kept on the prevention of faults in an exercise which is powerful and can therefore be dangerous.

Battements Frappés

Anatomically speaking, the faults in battements frappés have no special origin. The difficulties are inherent in the movement itself. This also applies to *Petits battements sur le cou de pied* when the tendency to sickle-in or out is more apparent. The slight outward turn of the foot can only be taken correctly if the *knee* is well turned out. Otherwise a true sickling-out (abduction) in the forepart of the foot will result, looking deceptively like the correct position, but harmful instead of valuable.

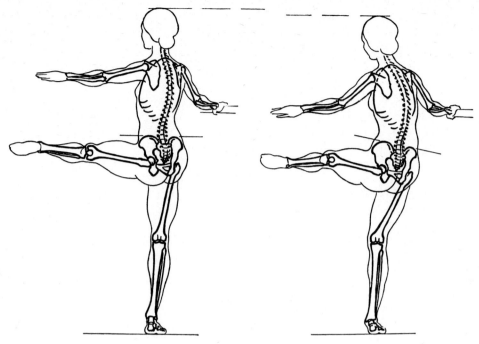

Fig. 34. COMMON FAULTS IN DÉVELOPPÉ EN AVANT
Note rolling foot, bent knee, twisted pelvis, rounded chest.

Développés

These are second only in importance to *pliés* in their influence on all subsequent movements and therefore they will be considered in the same detail. There are four parts to the movement.

1. The body is well lifted, the supporting hip well tucked in and the foot adjusted to its 3-point holding on the floor, whilst the foot of the working side is brought to the heel of the stationary foot pointed strongly, and with knee pressed outward.
2. The moving foot travels up the side of the supporting leg, finishing, according to the school of thought, either at the side of the supporting knee, or just in front.
3. The leg is stretched into the required position.
4. The leg is lowered on to the toe and drawn inward by the *battement tendu* movement to the required finish.

Various *ports de bras* accompany the leg movements. There are many opportunities for mistakes in execution. Some of them are subtle and are a matter of style rather than anatomy. Others are more definitely muscular or structural.

1. First and foremost should the correctness of the supporting side be watched. Many subsequent mistakes begin here.

2. In young children the foot of the moving leg will want to sickle-in. It is an ugly but not harmful mistake and, mechanically speaking, will correct itself more quickly if the knee is well pressed out.

3. When the leg is carried forward, two things may happen: (*a*) The pelvis will twist and the hip move forward on the side of the moving leg. This, as we now know, is a rotation of the spine. But the more perfect the *développé*, the less will the spine move in any direction and the more will the movement be localised to the hip. "Pull in the hips," is the teachers' method of explaining this. The business of the spinal muscles is to keep the body erect.

(*b*) The supporting knee may bend. This is to relieve the pull of the hamstring muscles, as in *grands battements*. Two things then happen. Either the weight of the body falls backward behind the supporting leg, and to keep the upright position the head then pokes forward; or else the reverse movement takes place, and the trunk is bent forward and the chin tilted upwards.

There is another reason for this tendency to bend the supporting knee, and that is to bring certain accessory muscles into play to help sustain the weight of the raised leg in this position. If the movement is done correctly, the correct muscles will work. By repetition of the correct execution, the correct muscles will strengthen.

The difficulty of the last inch of straightening of the knee in a *développé en avant* may be due to tightness of the hamstring muscles so that the rectus femoris, the front thigh muscle which proclaims its load by pain and aching, has to work more strongly to effect the straightening. Short muscles on one side of a limb are stretched in many instances by strong contractions of their opposing groups more surely than in trying to stretch them by the forcible means sometimes adopted.

In 2nd position, there is another problem. Because the true outward rotation of the hip is limited, especially when the leg is raised to hip height, the pelvis wants to turn to ease the strain, and the movement can easily become what as far as the hips are concerned is virtually a *développé en avant*. Unless too, the lumbar spine is fully flexible, there will be an ugly twist of the pelvis, a fault often seen when the torso is long in proportion to the legs, but also when height is aimed at, at the expense of style. See Fig. 35.

Finally, the displacement of the body in 2nd position is greater than in 4th, and therefore the supporting side has to work more strongly in the hip joint to keep the body upright.

Développé derrière is full of difficulties, mainly because it requires extension in the hip joint far beyond the normal range of 15°. Supposing even 60° has been obtained by training, that is still insufficient for an arabesque or

Fig. 35. THE ARABESQUE

A. Correct alignment in arabesque.   B.   Incorrect alignment, shoulders and hips twisted, a fault
commonly met with in dancers with a long back, as in the illustration, but not by any means confined
to them.

attitude, and the remainder has to be obtained by extension of the lumbar
and thoracic spine.   In order that the leg should be carried well behind,
a certain degree of rotation of the spine is also necessary. This, perforce, must
come from the thoracic region, since it is absent from the lumbar.   Hence,
unless the rotation is limited to the lower thoracic vertebrae, the shoulder
girdle will take part in the rotation, resulting in a faulty position. Nothing but
correct effort can overcome these anatomical difficulties. (See Chapter V.)

From this point onwards, save for the inherent and always present difficulty
of the turned hip, the reason for the commonly found faults are merely repetition
of what has already been described, until we come to "*sur les pointes*".

Sur les pointes

Any fault in this, the unique possession of the ballet dancer, is important,
since any fault very quickly produces damage, whereas with absolutely correct
technique, a dancer can use her "*pointes*" for thirty years with no ill effect. (See
Fig. 54.)

Undoubtedly the shape of the foot is of importance, but nevertheless, if the
dancer is trained correctly, the weight of the body is held and distributed in
such a way that the minimum falls upon the toes.

First and foremost is the need for absolutely correct "placing" of the body.
This means all that has already been said on the subject in Chapter XI, the
automatic holding of the spine at its longest, the ribs stretched, the head held
without tension, the hip muscles tight and, above all, the *knees absolutely straight*.
So much for the body.

With a high arch, such as shown Fig. 28c, the foot is usually soft and flexible
and needs more preparatory training than one more tightly knit (see Fig. 28A).
This training is given in the *terre à terre* work which uses the small muscles of

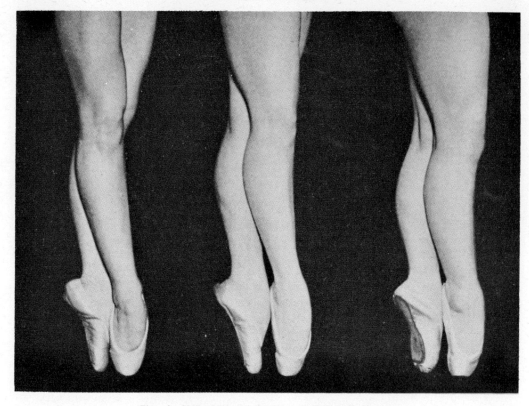

Fig. 36. SUR LES POINTES—FIFTH POSITION

the foot, and also in those movements which require pressure on, and resistance from, the floor—such as *battements tendus* and *frappés*. The highly arched foot is more apt to sickle in or out—both dangerous faults "*sur les pointes*", for the reason that has been shown in Chapter VII. An additional danger is that the ankle joint has lost the safeguard of muscles which, on the *demie pointe*, can quickly adjust to changing positions; on the full *pointe* they are themselves in a fixed position and cannot, therefore, move. These muscles offer excellent support so long as no alteration is made in the knee or ankle joint; in fact, they practically splint the limb. Therefore it is most important that the "splints" are correctly adjusted on the limb in its new position. If the foot sickles out, (see Fig. 37c) the weight of the body, instead of falling directly through the knee and ankle to the floor, will be diverted to the inner side of the foot, stretching ligaments and muscles beyond their power to maintain the arch, and above all, putting additional weight on the side of the big toe and so displacing it, with the resultant hallux valgus. "Sickling-in" (Fig. 37A) on the pointe is not so damaging to the foot, but stretches the lateral ligaments of the ankle and leaves the foot vulnerable to sprain by a sudden turning over.

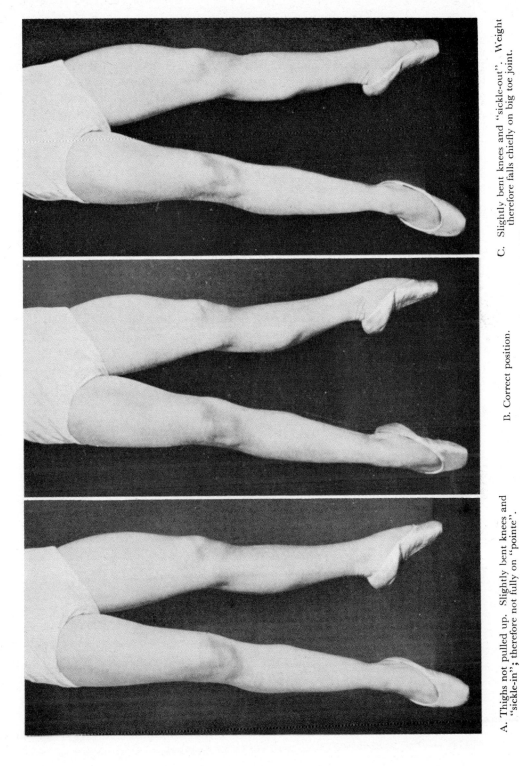

A. Thighs not pulled up. Slightly bent knees and "sickle-in"; therefore not fully on "pointe".

B. Correct position.

C. Slightly bent knees and "sickle-out". Weight therefore falls chiefly on big toe joint.

Fig. 37. SUR LES POINTES—SECOND POSITION

A final fault—and one often seen—is the drawing together of the toes in 5th position. Anatomically speaking, and apart from any school of thought in the ballet world, the floor space between the toes is correct since it leaves the alignment of foot to leg correct. If the toes are drawn together there must be an over action of the muscles which act on the forefoot in plantar flexion; this creates difficulties of balance and of making a smooth beginning, for example in *bourrées*, and is certainly liable to harden and make bulkier the calf muscles.

Of the years of training which should precede any attempt at *pointe* work, nothing more can be added beyond perhaps the warning that the bones of the tarsus do not ossify and become true bone until 7–8 years old (and for many years after the bones continue to become harder). Before that age, they are soft and easily distorted. *Pointe* work, as we have said, is the unique possession of the ballet dancer and should be treasured by her. The child who has taken the audience of admiring relatives and friends by storm at the annual display is little better for the applause, and will certainly not value it if, as a young woman, she is unable to find shoes to accommodate the painful enlarged toe joints which appeared long after she had forgotten all about the clapping, but which began their career as a result of injury invisible at that time. So read again the chapters on the foot and, teachers, lend them to those mothers who will not listen to your counsel.

CHAPTER XIII

STRESSES AND STRAINS

When we consider what is demanded of the framework of the body from the time of the first lesson at the *barre* to the appearance of the dancer on the stage, it is not surprising that from time to time there should be mishaps, and that protesting muscles, joints and ligaments should occasionally give trouble. Provided that the pupil has no structural defects, speaking from the point of view of ballet training, up to about twelve years of age complaints of aches and pains are normally trivial. During the teens and with the advent of *pointe* work, they are liable to need more consideration, and of course with the heavy time-table of the professional dancer, and at times the modern choreographer's sublime disregard for the limitations of the human body, injuries, as apart from strain, are more likely to occur. Nevertheless they are rare in proportion to the number of performers and performances involved, and though it may seem, as we list the possibilities, that ballet is a dangerous career leaving in its trail a long list of casualties, in actual fact the record both for fitness and freedom from disabling mishaps in a ballet company is extremely good, and this in spite of the long hours of work and rehearsals, irregular meals and lack of fresh air.

There are a certain number of typical stresses and strains that may be found in any ballet school, or indeed in classes for amateurs who often go beyond merely elementary work. Some of these undoubtedly would not be heard of were every pupil perfectly constructed for ballet training, or even if those with special and similar difficulties could be taught together. Short of this idealistic conception of the classroom, however, some precautions can be taken if the teacher is aware of the make-up of each pupil. This entails that she should teach the children at intervals in bare feet or open sandals and at the most a bathing slip only. Children are intelligent little creatures about their own bodies and can be shown quite young how to work with special relation to their own physical problems.

As might be expected feet figure more largely amongst complaints in the ballet class than anything else, knees running a close second. In young children they are mostly transient. For instance, pain along the inner border of the foot when standing at the *barre* will most likely be found to be due to the effort of correcting a "roll" (assuming, of course, that the turn-out is not being forced). It is not important unless it persists. If after a day or two it has not disappeared, it is better to take the child off work for a few days. Many children correct rolling feet with no resulting discomfort, but in the exception persistent pain indicates that the ligaments of the foot are feeling the strain of adjusting to the new position, and ligaments in the foot are quicker to react and slower to recover from strain than are muscles. This will often be so in the highly arched foot where the muscles are not sufficiently strong and undue work falls upon the ligaments in standing. In parenthesis it may be pointed out that it is perhaps more important than in any other type, that flexible highly arched feet should be trained from the very beginning to hold the correct position on the floor, ball of big toe, ball of little toe and heel, since it is one way of strengthening the muscles of the sole of the foot which have such an important part to play in maintaining the arch, and which tend to be weak in the foot which is beautiful to look at but is not inherently strong. If in such, during the first few years persistent "rolling" is left unchecked, we have the soft mobile foot that gives way on *pointe*, and has no push off in elevation.

Apart from the pain along the inner side of the foot, various small aches may be found in young children for which a couple of days' rest from class is usually all that is needed. It is not always possible to locate exactly the site of a strain in a structure so bound together by ligaments as is the foot. As work becomes advanced there are more possibilities of pressure here or a pull there, and if such arise the most helpful procedure is to find the exact position or exercise that produces it. Eliminating this for a few days is often all that is required, and perhaps working in a light bandage when including it again in class. The elastic net type of bandage is more suitable than crêpe for this purpose, giving sufficient support, without bulk or undue restriction of movement. Should the pain be persistent, then other treatment may be needed.

Strains of ligaments in the foot are felt mostly on the supporting foot, i.e. in weight bearing, and in springs, less so in holding *en l'air* or in such movements as *battements frappés*, *battements tendus* and so on. There are one or two muscles which may also be the source of trouble, but the pain will then be felt on movement rather than in standing and especially when on *pointe*. The usual place that the dancer will point to is just behind the inner ankle. It occurs most often in the highly arched foot with loose ankle joint and it is fairly safe to say that it is produced by some degree, however small, of "sickling out" either on *pointe* or in other exercises or positions. It is especially necessary to deal with the cause, which harks back to faulty technique, for this strain may become a tiresome and recurring inflammation in the tendon of the muscle concerned, the Tibialis Posterior. (See page 40.) Having come down the outer side of the leg, its tendon winds round the inner ankle, spreading out into smaller tendons under the foot. Its action is to point the foot and to turn up the inner border. The stretch put upon the main tendon then is obvious if the foot is sickled out, more especially when weight bearing. The fact that this particular strain is mostly found in the more delicate type of foot reminds us that strength and flexibility rarely go hand in hand, and it is important to work for the building up of strength in the naturally mobile type. As we have already said nothing is more important to the over-flexible foot than the correct use of the resistance of the floor. It is too easy for its owner to neglect this, showing the end result of e.g. a *battement tendu* without the strong slide of the foot on the floor before arching the foot, and in steps of elevation—*assemblés*, etc.—the same tendency. It is in part at least the reason for the better elevation in the dancer who has had to work to produce a good arch than in the one who is by nature so endowed.

There is one other tendon which can give trouble, the Achilles tendon which joins the calf muscles to the heel. The complaint is either a pain above the heel in *pliés* and *fondus* or when pointing the foot; and at a later stage on turning the foot upward. It may be caused by lack of a good *demi-plié* especially with a stiff type of foot, or if there exists a short Achilles tendon. Whatever the cause, all work should be stopped at once and advice sought, as neglected, it can be one of the most disabling of the dancer's strains, becoming in time a real synovitis, with creaking in the tendon and severe pain.

These strains of ligaments and tendons that have been mentioned do not of course exhaust all possibilities that may occur in the classroom. They cover the main types which are due to the nature of the work, rather than any extraneous cause. In addition there is of course the ordinary sprained ankle, ruptured fibres in the calf muscle and in the Achilles tendon. These last two are never met in younger students. They belong to the adult dancer and need immediate medical attention. The sprained ankle may occur at almost any age, but it is an injury rather than a strain. In its mild form a very few days' rest from work is all that is necessary, but should it be severe it is quite a serious injury. The common site of damage is in the lateral ligament on the outer side of the ankle, divided into three bands of which the front or middle one is the most likely to suffer damage, either by overstretching or the rupture of a few of the fibres. The result is pain which can be intense, swelling which comes up within a few minutes, and bruising sometimes well up the leg. In a severe case there is always the chance of a small fracture of the lower end of the fibula, or of the 5th metatarsal bone, for which reason no doubt the doctor in charge would secure an X-ray. A fracture, if present, would delay return to work but would not leave any permanent damage. The ankle is a good healer and the victim of this injury need not feel that it will not be as good as ever in a relatively short time. To any exercises which may be given at the clinic, the dancer can add with advantage those of her own which use the joint fully without weight-bearing, such as *battements frappés*, and *battements tendus;* and later gentle *relevés*, *demi-pliés* and so on. As soon as possible a return to class is advisable, but, *pointe* work should be omitted until all swelling has disappeared. The sufferer from this injury may take comfort from the fact that for any residue of pain that may persist, there is no better treatment for it than a good session at the *barre*.

The actual bones of the feet rarely figure on the casualty list but yet the author has come across two cases which would be considered rare, one in a girl of twelve years old and another of fourteen. There is such a thing as a spontaneous fracture of one of the long bones of the forefoot, arising from no known cause and presenting as symptoms pain and swelling over the front of the

5

foot. It may keep the child off work for a month or more, but eventually training can be continued without any after effects.

One other minor condition that occurs occasionally is an extra growth of bone at the back of the heel. The heel becomes red and a soft bursa may form from the friction of the shoe. Indeed the whole condition may be caused by just that, so that it is important to examine all the footwear in use, including ballet shoes and the exact place the ribbons contact the heel when tied. With the relief of all pressure, including a protective pad if necessary, the swelling may subside, but otherwise the exostosis as it is called may have to be dealt with surgically.

Finally come complaints of pressure pain under the heel, or under the big toe. It may be caused merely by a hard ballet shoe and this should be investigated first. It is especially bad for a hard ridge of the shoe to be allowed to press into the soft flesh under the ball of the foot, as in an extreme case inflammation of the sesamoid bones embedded in the tendon of the muscles can be set up. These small bones do not become fully hardened until well on in the teens, and inflammation in them can be difficult to cure and result in leaving the foot unsuitable for training. This is a rare occurrence but not unknown.

Eliminating this source we come to the pain which is the precurser of the occupational hazard of the ballet dancer, *hallux valgus*. The first symptom may be pain on the under side of the big toe or on the outer, either on standing and especially when on *demi-pointe*. The immediate question that arises is not about the toe but about the shoes in use. For ballet children more than any it is of paramount importance that *all* footwear should leave room for *all* the toes. The slightest shortening is sufficient to start off this trouble, the slightest lack of width at the toe end is enough to press the big toe towards the centre of the foot. Appearance is of secondary importance to the urgent necessity that there should be room for the toes to grow in the natural direction, with no pressure on any, especially on the big toe. And socks or stockings must be equally carefully watched. Two or three months' growth in a young child may necessitate replacements for both, and no economic reasons must stand in the way, hard though it may be. This is the first investigation to be made when a child complains of pain under or around the big toe joint, remembering that boys are no less immune from this trouble than girls if wrongly shod. All shoes, outdoor, indoor, ballet and even bedroom slippers should be examined. A very early *hallux valgus* may correct itself when given foot space inside the shoes. At a later stage little can be done for it.

One often finds in the early signs of pain around the big toe that the pupil has the very bad habit of curling her toes in *barre* exercises, a fault difficult to detect in shoes, but detrimental if persisted in, and a very bad introduction to *pointe* work, in which the straight big toe is of prime importance. The child with the highly arched foot and the one with little arch are both apt to cultivate this habit of clutching, the first because she cannot otherwise feel her toes and the second in the mistaken impression that it will improve the arch. The result is an imbalance in the pull of the two systems of muscles which preserve the straightness of the toes, and loss of that strength which is needed for both springs and *pointe* work. It is not unlikely that this has some bearing on the incidence of *hallux valgus*, but whether or no, it should be checked as likely to lead to other troubles. Once the big toe joint has become deflected it is impossible to cure but careful and correct technique is the best insurance against any progression of the condition. Other than this it is important to keep the joint entirely flexible and to remember that teen-agers, succumbing to the lure of fashion shoes with high heels which throw the weight of the body on to the front of the foot, and with narrow fronts which cramp the toes, are sacrificing the serviceability of their feet for allure, and giving every opportunity for the big toe to become a trouble maker.

One other difficulty with the big toe may be mentioned. It is less common than *hallux valgus* and the pain is felt almost exclusively on the *demi-pointe*. This is known as *hallux rigidus* and as its name implies, it is a stiffening of the joint due to some arthritic increase of growth in the bones. It is more painful in action than is the *valgus* deviation but does not increase with the same speed. A *very* mild degree may be kept under with the aid of some form of heat treatment and the stoicism which is characteristic of the ballet dancer, but a severe case should be referred to the orthopaedic surgeon, since the results of operation are more likely to restore the foot to a usable (dancing) condition than in the case of *hallux valgus*

As has been said earlier, knees are second only to feet as a source of trouble. They have a tremendous amount of hard work from the very beginning. They are vulnerable and unforgiving joints. An ankle will recover from quite severe injury with no after-effects but the knee has a long memory and any real damage to it can be a major calamity.

Injuries or inflammatory conditions fall roughly into two classes, those which affect the ligaments and cartilages and those in which the patella is involved. The former are the most common and the earliest complaints come from the very junior children and are usually due to nothing more than an excess of zeal in pulling up the thighs, which action of course draws up the patella. The resulting pain may be well above the knee or just below (Fig. 38) and is caused by a slight stretch on the tendon of the muscle on the front of the thigh which pulls up the patella, or upon the ligament by which the patella is attached to the tibia below. It is as well to give the child a day or two off work, when the pain should disappear, and a warning to avoid any jerking in straightening the knees when back at the *barre*.

Apart from this small strain, others depend very largely on the formation of the knees in relation to the thigh and leg. A knee which is in good alignment rarely gives any trouble. By far the greater number of troubles occur amongst those pupils with any marked degree of knock-knee, those with short hamstring muscles who therefore do not straighten the joint without effort, and

definitely those with any hyperextension or "sway-back" at the knee joint.   In
the first of these, the knock-kneed, there is often some laxness in the joint, with
resulting instability and a lack of a perfect balance in the working of muscles
and ligaments on either side which control and produce movement.   In
addition, the tibia is slightly out-turned, rendering it easy for the child to turn

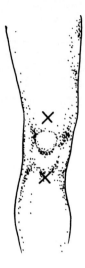

Fig. 38.   SITE OF PAIN DUE TO "PULLING UP" THIGH
MUSCLES TOO FORCIBLY

out from below the knee instead of from the hip, a fruitful source both of foot
and knee strain.

When a child points definitely to the inner or outer side of the knee as the
pain-giving spot it is a signal for caution.   The inner side especially is the
most commonly met site of strain of the ligament, and later of a nipping or
displaced cartilage.   Before thinking so far ahead, however, it is wise to
make sure that the cause does not lie nearer at hand, in fact at the first exercise
at the *barre*.   *Pliés* are a tax on the knee even when perfectly performed, more
especially in the upward movement.   Any falling inwards of the knees at the
moment of rising puts a great strain on the inner side of the joints and this is
doubled when there is any relaxation or "sitting" at the lowest point.   This
fault is injurious to the feet, but much more so to the knees, and repeated
continually may easily be the source of strain on the ligaments.

In neither of these strains do we find swelling, but in a third condition the
knee is puffy and stiff, due to inflammation in the bursa or sac of fluid which
acts as a buffer between the patella and the tibia.   It is more likely to be the
result of prolonged kneeling, or in boys from crashing down on to one knee,
than from straight work, and if it does not subside speedily advice should be
obtained without delay.

Any condition in which a knee locks should be regarded as needing
immediate investigation, as also should that in which it gives way suddenly.
Either may recover temporarily, but should nevertheless be taken as warnings,

and the possibility be eliminated of a cartilage nipping or a patella slipping. Pain which is felt either over or under the patella, more when the knee is flexed than when straight, needs an accurate diagnosis of the cause for fear of inflammation of the under surface of the patella, a condition which if it exists would be likely to put an end to further training. One cannot say why this arises, other than over-use of a joint predisposed to such a condition, perhaps by former injury which has not been divulged at the time of the audition. Parents and children are apt to forget the incidence of an accident in early years, or maybe have a reluctance to confess to such. Remember too that any infective illness may leave potential joint trouble, which might not become manifest under ordinary life conditions, but which will be awakened by the unusual demands of ballet. This is especially so in the case of the knee joint. These are rare eventualities, fortunately, but they do occasionally occur, again more often in the knee which is not in perfect alignment with the thigh.

The next area of trouble is not in a joint but in the muscles on the inner side of the thigh (Fig. 39), caused by the stretch that is required of them in all movements *à la seconde*. There is a corresponding pain recognised as "rider's strain" due to a similar pull. In dancers it may become very persistent and is found in quite young pupils as well as in the seasoned. There is no better method of invoking it than rushing to the *barre* and practising limbering exercises with leg raised on the *barre* before the lesson, instead of when the body is thoroughly warmed up. It can, however, arise without this culpable behaviour. It is caused by a few fibres of the muscle concerned having been overstretched or possibly torn at some time, and in the healing process they have become, as it were, matted together. They need therefore to be

Fig. 39. SITE OF "RIDER'S STRAIN"

separated again and there are various treatments advocated to this end. Before resorting to them it is worth while trying self-help in the form of exercises which put a stretch on the painful spot. Thorough warming first is essential, either by a hot bath or by local heat. The victim should then put herself in a position when the pain is just noticeable and from this perform *gently* and *rhythmically* stretching movements to the limit of endurance. Such a position might well be one in which the leg is raised in second position on a low *barre* and the supporting leg bent and stretched alternately to get a further stretch on the painful thigh. Or the exercise could begin in a lunge position, both feet on the floor, swinging from side to side by bending the knees alternately; but the most favourable position can often be found by the performer. The essence of this cure . . . and it is astonishingly efficacious . . . is slow rhythmic movement, and persistence, in spite of a temporary increase of pain and in spite of its intensity, over a period varying from a few days to a month. The author has found it remarkably effective even in pain of long standing for which much more serious measures have been advocated.

This pain is quite distinct from a catch or click which besets some students in the mid or later teens in performing the unfolding of the leg in *developpés* and which is confined almost exclusively to that movement, is felt in the groin but is sometimes referred to the region of the hip, though not in fact affecting the hip joint itself. Its exact cause is difficult to determine, but it wears off in time and though uncomfortable need not cause the dancer any concern.

The hip joint as such is peculiarly free from trouble in spite of the abnormal work that falls upon it in ballet, but the lower back may have its quota. One does not meet complaints of pain in this region until well on in the teens, providing the structure of the body is normal and well proportioned. Those most prone to aches or pains are those with long backs and the tight hips which often go with them. Boys of this build may find lifts responsible for some discomfort if not definite pain, and in both girls and boys of an earlier age the effort to achieve a high *arabesque* or long holdings in *adagio, arabesques, attitudes* and their variants may be the starting point of pressure between the lumbar vertebrae. The strain may be transferred to the sacro-iliac joints, that meeting place of the sacrum (Figs. 1, 2) and the pelvic bone known as the ilium. Unless the pain is disabling a few days' rest can be allowed to see if it will disappear, and then any fault in the "placing" of the body carefully checked. It may be that the dancer is holding the upper part too vertical in *grands battements derrière* at the *barre* and in other exercises in fourth position *derrière en l'air*, or striving for greater flexibility than the type of back will allow. Boys may need some special strengthening exercises for the shoulders before continuing with "lifts". Or it may be that the dancer is overtired and needs rest. The spine is apt to register this need more quickly than any other part of the body.

We have covered some of the aches and pains that are typical in the training of the dancer. That there will always be others is inevitable in combining the complexity of the human body with the complexity of ballet technique. But as has already been stressed, the closer the physique conforms to the ideal, the less the hazard of strain in any part. Thorough warming up, perfect execution of *barre* work and good food rank high amongst insurance against injuries. All three are sometimes neglected. Nothing starts the circulation of the whole body more quickly than *pliés* at the *barre*, performed with meticulous care and concentration, yet it is not unknown for the boredom of endless repetition to creep in as the years go by, and for these most fundamental exercises to be done with the minimum instead of the maximum effort. It is also not unknown for a late comer to the class to do a few perfunctory exercises at the *barre* and then join in at a stage when the body ought to be thoroughly warm; and to perform the simplest limbering or stretching from cold is begging for trouble.

Correct execution, the second safeguard, can only come by degrees, but certain subtle errors can be checked from the very beginning. The troubles that may arise from the rolling or sickling foot have already been mentioned, as those also from the inturned hip, the straining for height rather than line in *adagio* and so on. There is another technical fault which is common and often overlooked, viz. the habit of keeping the weight entirely on the supporting foot during the *barre* exercises. The failure to relax the muscles by transferring the weight on to *both* feet in that momentary pause between one movement and the next is a factor in muscles becoming bulky, hard and inelastic—and so liable to injury—and it is one of the nuances in teaching that can easily be overlooked. The alternation of stretching and relaxing in muscular action is the greatest of all safeguards against strain and it is beautifully exemplified in ballet technique when correctly performed. Apart from increasing the bulk, it is possible that the bad habit of omitting the momentary relaxation between movements may also be the cause of cramp to which some pupils are prone— in the foot muscles and in the thighs. For them especially it is worth checking up on this point.

Good food, the third on our list of preventives, raises the problem of the teen-ager who puts on weight and girth, to combat which she is afraid of her naturally good appetite and begins to diet. To tell her at this stage that she will thin down again later is no comfort. She persists in her fasting, loses weight and energy and finds she is not as strong on her *pointes* as she used to be, or that her back aches or that she has a pain here and another one there and goes off for various treatments when what she is needing is nourishment.* Naturally the diet for a dancer must be arranged with certain reservations, stodgy puddings eliminated in favour of fruit and salads, the intake of sugar, starches and fats modified, but any serious dieting should only be undertaken under medical supervision, and it is rarely necessary. A sudden and definite increase of bulk in the early teens may often be counteracted by cutting off one or even two classes a week, giving muscles which are overloaded with fatigue products

* It may be noted that this state of affairs is not confined to teen-agers.

the opportunity to eliminate them. Indeed, for more reasons than one it might possibly be of advantage if the training could be slowed down during the years between say fourteen and sixteen, when the changes of adolescence and the pressure of general education are making great demands on the physical and nervous system of the child. The increase of energy and vitality after this age is very noticeable in the ballet classroom and one wonders whether anything would ultimately be lost if a somewhat less intensive training were to precede it. The long slow building up of the body until it attains the strength, endurance, flexibility, speed, the refinement and the beauty which we almost take for granted in the tremendous technique of the ballet dancer is both a science and an art. It cannot be hurried—and it is never finished.

CHAPTER XIV

QUESTIONS AND ANSWERS

Teachers are often confronted with problems not belonging entirely to
anatomy, but which are on the borderline between normal and abnormal
growth. In order to deal with some of these questions (all of which have
come from teachers themselves) this chapter has been added and the answers
given in a practical and non-technical form. The reader is asked to forgive
some repetition of important points. It is really only in the orthopaedic
department of a hospital that true insight can be gained into the problems
of the deviations of the growth and structure of the body. In the absence of
this, however, the following may be of help.

I. AT WHAT AGE SHOULD A CHILD BEGIN BALLET?

A question that is often asked, and which has been answered by at least
one great teacher, Maestro Cecchetti, who puts the age not earlier than
8 years. He is wise, for until the eighth year the bones of the foot are not fully
fully ossified; neither is the knee strong enough to be trained. Indeed, for
many years, until the twenty-fifth actually, the whole skeleton continues its
bony consolidation.

Between eight and twelve years old a limited amount of work only should be
permitted and that most carefully supervised. How often does one hear of the
beginners' class being handed over to the youngest member of the staff, whereas
it is really a task for the most experienced.

There is, however, another and very important aspect of this problem. In
recent years, much greater recognition has been given to the physical, as well as
to the artistic value of ballet training, and in a few schools it is even included in
the curriculum. There is no doubt that teachers could further this appreciation
by using their work educationally—which, in the real sense means artistically.
Teachers of school subjects employ methods nowadays which are the outcome
of study, *not only of their subject, but of the child.* Especially is this so in the
kindergarten and the lower school, where *results* are not the primary aim. Is
the teacher of ballet in line in this respect? Ballet is essentially an adult
conception of movement. The child's expression is less co-ordinated and less
sophisticated. Stylised movement forced on to the immature body and mind by
a technique in advance of his development may have harmful results, not only
physically but in subtler directions—in character, temperament and the more
elusive realm of the spirit, driving underground, perhaps for ever, the potential
artist in the child. It must be remembered that the child is not an adult in
miniature. He passes through many stages of development before reaching

73

maturity and in the hands of a good educationalist he is given the appropriate tools with which to express his changing outlook at each stage. Thus the teacher of painting does not supply him with fine pencils and small brushes at the beginning, and ask for an exact reproduction of the objects to be portrayed. He is allowed to use tools more easily manipulated, and to express his understanding of things as he sees them, in a language peculiarly his own. Not until 9–10 years of age is he asked to learn any technique. Should not the teaching of ballet in some measure correspond? Would anything be lost and would not much be gained, both physically and artistically, by this more enlightened attitude to the child, an attitude which has justified itself beyond question where it has been applied, and which Cecchetti well understood; for indeed, although he says not earlier than 8 years, he adds that according to nationality and climate, he would advocate as late as 10 years for the beginning.

Teachers of young children would perhaps find it interesting to read the more elementary books on child psychology—such as *The Natural Development of the Child* by A. Bowley, published by E. & S. Livingstone Ltd. It includes an excellent bibliography for further reading.

2. AT WHAT AGE SHOULD A CHILD BEGIN *pointe* WORK?

This question has already been touched upon in the previous chapter, but it is of such paramount importance that it is worth while to enlarge further on the subject.

Although the recognition of the danger of too early *pointe* work is far more widely accepted than a few years ago, it is still possible to buy blocked shoes to fit a six-year-old and to find classes where they are allowed to wear them. It cannot be too strongly stressed that *pointe* work is the end result of slow and gradual training of the whole body, back, hips, thighs, legs, feet, co-ordination of movement and the "placing" of the body, so that the weight is lifted upwards off the feet, with straight knees, perfect balance, with a perfect *demi-pointe*, and without any tendency on the part of the feet to sickle either in or out or the toes to curl or clutch. This moment will arrive at different times in different children, not only by virtue of previous training but according to their physical type, and in this may be included the growth of the bones. All the bones of the body begin as a relatively soft material known as cartilage which becomes progressively ossified into true bone at different times, being completed as late as twenty-five years. During this period there is a gradual hardening from the centre outward. In the long bones, such as those of the leg, forefoot and toes, the shaft ossifies first, the ends known as the epiphyses remaining connected to the shaft only by cartilage until the early teens, with considerable variation as between one child and another as to the exact time at which the cartilage becomes bony. Ideally, if *pointe* work could be delayed until this time in children with poor bone structure, no doubt their feet would be safeguarded, but this is a counsel of perfection, the most that can be done is to

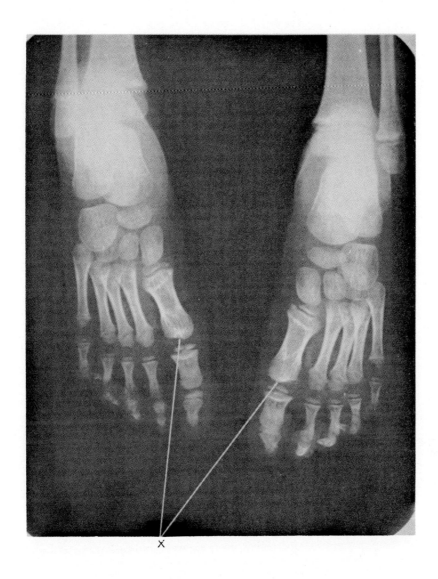

X

Fig. 40. AN X-RAY OF 4 YEAR OLD FEET

X Note the big space filled with soft cartilage between the bones of the forefoot and those of the toes; and the epiphyses of the bones of the toes, appearing as flat discs and separated from the main shaft.

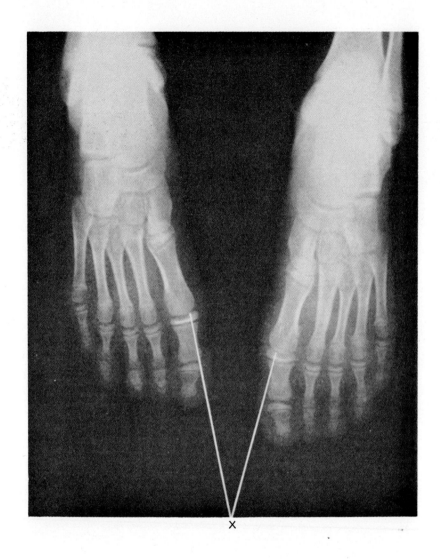

Fig. 41. FEET AT 11 YEARS

X Note the forefoot bones are now less widely separated from the toes, but the epiphyses
are still not joined to the shaft of the bones of the toes.

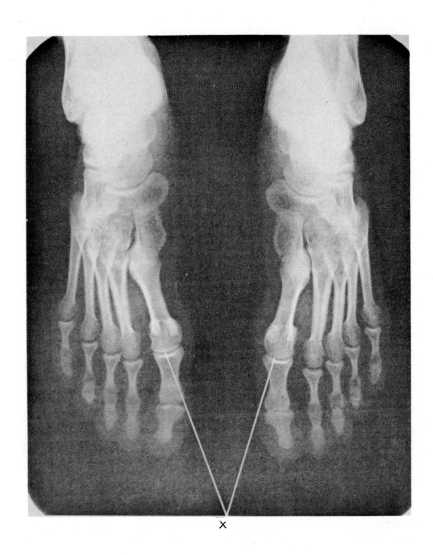

X

Fig. 42.   FEET AT 19 YEARS

X The bones of the toes are now in one piece and the space between the forefoot and toe bones is finally reduced. (Note also in this illustration there is a small degree of *hallux valgus*, showing the typical displacement of the upper end of the first metatarsal bone.)

prepare the whole body as perfectly as possible, and to ensure that the introduction of the work on *pointe* is slow and gradual, rarely earlier than twelve
years of age and preferably later. The fact that some feet can be found to have
survived the abuse of tottering around on blocked shoes from the age of six
onwards is no criterion as to its safety. The author has met at least one case of
a child whose strong feet were unharmed by "dancing" on *pointe* at six years
old, but who succumbed later with knee trouble. There is little doubt that
the strain had been resisted by the feet but had been transferred to the knee
joints.

The further question is, however, should a child do any *pointe* work unless
she is taking her dancing professionally? The once-a-week class can never be a
suitable preparation for *pointe* work, and what is gained by including it? On
the other hand, a risk is being taken which may result in lifelong disability.
The teacher does not see the results. The child gives up her lessons as other
things claim her and if, maybe years later (for damage does not always show
at once), she has foot, knee or back trouble, she goes to a doctor for advice, not
to her one-time teacher. The doctor, then, rightly enough, condemns ballet
and is unable to do much to repair the damage.

With the child who is going to train professionally it is different. Her
training will be systematic and concentrated, and, just as every profession has
its risks, this is one which has to be taken. In honesty one must say there is a
fair amount of enlargement of the big toe in ballet dancers, but only in a slight
degree and not to cause any great trouble; on the other hand, many dancers
have no foot trouble at all, as can be seen in Fig. 54. It seems to depend a
good deal on the type of foot.

3. SHOULD A CHILD WITH KNOCK-KNEES TRAIN FOR BALLET?

The shape of the pelvis and position of the thigh is an important factor in
determining the straightness of the legs as a whole. If the slope inwards is
exaggerated, either because of the width of the pelvis, or as sometimes happens,
an unusually small angle at the upper end of the femur, there will result the
condition we recognise as knock-knees.

A small degree of this may be considered normal in girls—due as pointed
out earlier, to the naturally wider pelvis and consequent greater slope inwards
of the thigh than in boys. The simplest test can be made, back view for choice,
by standing the child with feet only very slightly turned out, knees just touching.
There should normally then be not more than 1 inch between the heels
(allowing that a chubby child may still have a certain amount of fat between
the thighs which would prevent the knees closing completely). It is important
that this test should be made with *very* little turn-out as otherwise the inner
condyles of the femur—which may be large at this age and smaller in proportion later on—will prevent the heels from coming together and give a
false impression as to the degree of knock-knee existing.

How much greater mal-alignment may be permitted is a matter for

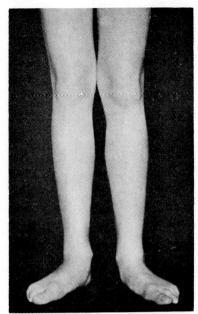

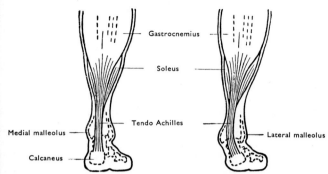

Fig. 44. NORMAL FOOT

BACK VIEW OF FOOT
IN Fig. 43
This is also seen when
Achilles tendon is short.

Fig. 43. KNOCK-KNEES WITH THE
TYPE OF FLAT FEET UNSUIT-
ABLE FOR THE BALLET CLASS

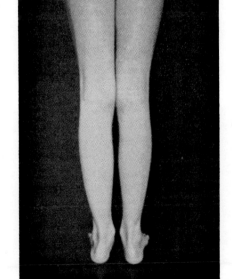

Fig. 45. KNOCK-KNEES, BACK VIEW
Showing a gap of 2 inches between the heels.
Anything greater than this will be a handicap in
advanced work. Note also rolling feet, nearly
always found in conjunction with this formation of
the legs.

balancing up the general physique against this particular disadvantage. The compact sturdy type can overcome a degree of knock-knee up to 2 inches but in no case is more than this desirable. In a thin tall child with poor musculature there is likely to be some slackness of the knee joint indicating weakness and the possibility of trouble later on. Moreover, there will be difficulty in acquiring speed, good elevation and strong *pointe* work since the thrust from the floor when knock-knees are present is taken, not in a straight line from foot to hip, but in one weakened by an angle at the knee joint and imposing a strain both on foot and knee. Markedly knock-knees with or without laxness in the joint may subsequently account for many of the ligamentous strains, slipped cartilages or various inflammations within the knee joint which are met from

A. Bow legs.   B. Can be held as an exercise but
                                      only a limited improvement can
                                      be permanently obtained.

Fig. 46.   BOW LEGS

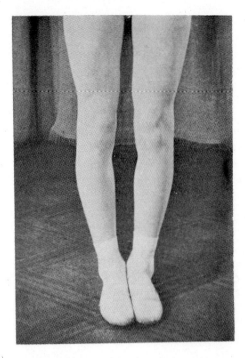

Fig. 46. BOW LEGS
C. A lesser degree of bow-legs which may improve but not be cured with training. Note in-turned knees and rolling of left foot.

time to time, and even for those strains of the foot, often difficult to locate accurately, which seem to arise for no obvious reason.

A word of warning must here be given against the hope that a child will outgrow knock-knees. A very young child may do so for the reason that the condition is due to unequal development of the two condyles of the femur, the inner having grown faster than the outer; a child, boy or girl, then appears startlingly knock-kneed at three and recovers completely by five years old, but the type that is met with at ten years old does not belong to this category.

4. CAN BOW-LEGS BE CURED BY BALLET?

There are two main types of bow legs. One is that in which the femur is normal but the tibia curves outward. An occasional boy may come up for audition with this formation but one does not find it amongst girls. Probably they have already been discouraged from learning ballet by a discriminating parent or teacher. The second type is met with in both sexes, though the degree is more marked in boys. In this the bowing includes the thighs so that when the feet are touching there is a space between the knees. This is not strictly a bowing of the legs. The space between the knees occurs by virtue of the fact that the curve of the femur instead of being situated on the front of the thigh has deviated somewhat to the outer side, thus changing the position of the condyles, which then face slightly inward instead of to the front, so causing the space between the knees (Fig. 46c). The real drawback to this formation lies

6

in the fact that the hip joint is always by nature in-turned and to that extent this type of bow leg interferes with perfect technical accomplishment; and of course it is ugly in girls and does not add to the charm of the male dancer. However, in the male one usually finds good elevation with some degree of bow leg, in girls it is more variable, depending on whether or no the position of the legs affects that of the feet. Again, as with knock-knees, it must not be imagined that training will correct the bowing. It can be disguised when the feet are both on the ground, close together, toes and heels touching and the whole limb rotated outward in the hips, so that momentarily the legs appear straight, but as soon as this effort is released they will return to the original position, after even twenty years of training; some slight improvement may however be obtained.

5. WHAT ADVICE HAVE YOU FOR TEACHING A CHILD WITH "SWAY-BACK" KNEES?

This may be a remnant of infantile bow-legs, with which it is often accompanied, in which the knees are pressed backward too far, leaving the ligaments at the back permanently stretched and the front of the knee too flat or almost hollow with a bulge above (Fig. 47). One sees this more often than formerly, which gives rise to the conjecture as to whether there may not also be a further cause, namely that the child with slight bow legs, or even without, has begun ballet too early, has been told to "pull up the thighs", and has responded by pressing back the knees, resulting in this sway-back position. Be that as it may the result is disastrous from the point of view of training, since the "placing" of the body is completely upset, the weight falling on the heels and any pulling up of the thighs increasing the trouble. Speed and elevation are affected and in a marked case of this kind it would be folly to accept the candidate. Even a very slight degree will need the careful adjustment of many exercises and a watchful eye from an experienced teacher. Perhaps the last criterion in the case of a promising child with this obstacle should be her intelligence to use the guidance that may be given her. In Figs. 48 and 49 can be seen this formation in a 12-year-old corrected in appearance by bringing the hip forward and the weight on to the front of the foot—a very difficult adjustment to make throughout every exercise and movement.

6. CAN A CHILD WHO CANNOT GET HER HEELS DOWN BECAUSE OF TIGHT TENDONS AT THE BACK EVER LOOSEN THEM?

The tendon at the back of the heel—the Achilles tendon—is a tough resistant structure. When the foot is straight forward the tightness does not affect it much. It means that the normal dorsiflexion of the foot is slightly diminished, and for walking, all that is required is a comfortable height of heel. But for ballet the full dorsiflexion is very important and in trying to get it, an oblique pull is made on the calcaneus with consequent rolling of the foot. It may be one of the reasons for incurable rolling. Persistent and long continued

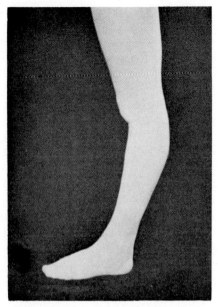

Fig. 47

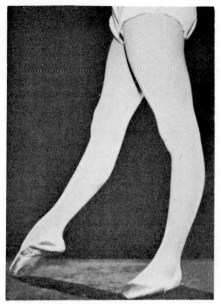

Fig. 48

Fig. 47. "SWAY-BACK" KNEES WITH
OVERDEVELOPED MUSCLE ABOVE,
PROBABLY THE RESULT OF
INFANTILE BOW-LEGS

Fig. 48. "SWAY-BACK" KNEES, POS-
SIBLY CAUSED BY PRESSING BACK
THE KNEES INSTEAD OF PULLING
UP THE THIGH MUSCLES

Fig. 49. APPEARANCE IMPROVED
BY ADJUSTMENT OF WEIGHT, A
CONTINUOUS EFFORT NOT POSSIBLE
TO SUSTAIN THROUGHOUT ALL
MOVEMENTS

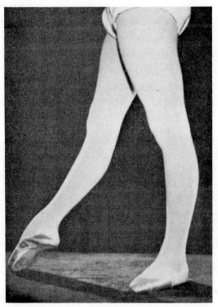

Fig. 49

work may stretch it a little but it is not an easy tendon to lengthen. Remember, the Achilles tendon is the tendon of the calf muscles, the action of which is pure plantar-flexion of the ankle. It can only be stretched by pure dorsiflexion, whether taken by bending the knee over the foot when the ankle joint is therefore in dorsiflexion, or by bending the foot itself upwards. If the relation of knee to foot is altered, as e.g. in extreme turning, the movement then is not pure and is of no use. In actual fact a short Achilles tendon is not really very common. It may appear short, or function as such through contraction in the calf muscles, and for remedy of this remember the value of *demi-pliés* and the returning of the weight on to both feet between all movements, however quickly taken and however brief the pause, remembering also that the *demi-plié* ends only at the point when the heels cannot hold the ground any longer. Apart from the classroom, however, it is worth bearing in mind that to walk about in too high heels, which keep the calf muscles in a state of contraction and the tendon at its shortest, is to make the task of stretching and relaxing calf muscles doubly difficult. If there is a true shortening, there is nothing to be done, except perhaps enjoy the good elevation that usually goes with it.

7. CAN TIGHT HAMSTRINGS BE STRETCHED?

The hamstring muscles are those situated on the back of the thigh, passing over the back of the knee. If they are tight, the child cannot fully stretch the knees, nor touch the ground with the fingers when bending forward. There was a vogue some years ago when the hall-mark of physical perfection seemed to be to touch the ground when bending forward. Tremendous efforts were made by people of all ages and shapes to achieve this end. Some fell into the hands of the doctor and it was shown that the continual pressure on the discs between the vertebrae which was inevitable in this downward bending had caused inflammation, particularly in people with short hamstrings. So that if these can be stretched at all—only in young children it is really possible—it should be done by a steady pull on the muscles themselves, one leg at a time, raised and fixed to the required height, whilst front thigh muscles are strongly contracted, i.e. knee kept absolutely straight. Especially dangerous is sitting with straight legs and bending forward to get the head on the knees, unless it can be done easily and without strain—when it is not necessary to do it!

8. IS BALLET GOOD FOR SPINAL CURVATURE?

This is a huge subject. By and large one would say that no child with a curvature is safe in the hands of a ballet teacher. It is commonly thought that a spinal curvature is a bending sideways of the spine but this is not really the case. A curvature is formed by the twisting of one vertebra upon the next. The muscles concerned in this are the deepest layer of short muscles going down the length of the spine. Their action is not completely understood and certainly no exercises can be located to them. This twisting of one vertebra on the next results in an alteration in the shape of the ribs which, it will be remembered, articulate with the vertebrae. A bony alteration of this kind is an alteration in structure and cannot be dealt with by any exercises, nor, as is sometimes claimed, by manipulation (as X-ray photographs taken before and after such treatment will easily confirm). All that can be done is to improve the general posture of the child or to resort to the orthopaedic surgeon.

This posture improvement must be done most carefully. Curvatures have an alarming way of increasing very quickly if the flexibility of the spine outruns the strength. A slight curve may in three months become a severe deformity if this should happen; so that the answer to this question is: "Do not take on responsibility for a condition which even those equipped to deal with it view with anxiety."

Many children, however, have some small degree of asymmetry of the body. One shoulder will appear a little higher than the other, the line of the torso to the waist will not be the same on the one side as the other and the points of the ears and shoulder blades are not level (Fig. 51). There may be some structural reason for this, possibly one leg a fraction longer than the other, or there may be some slight irregularity in the vertebrae of the spine. The latter can be checked by asking the child to bend downward as far as possible, head tucked in towards the knees.

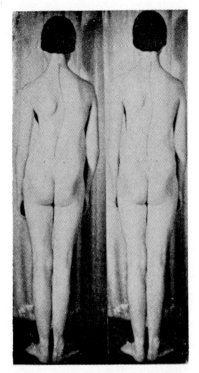

Fig. 50. NO CHANGE IN STRUC-TURE. IN SPITE OF THE IM-PROVEMENT IN POSTURE THIS CURVATURE SUBSEQUENTLY INCREASED VERY MARKEDLY.

In this position there should be no sign of a bulge of the ribs on the one side nor any flattening on the other; one shoulder blade should not appear more prominent than the other and there should be no sign of the muscles in the lower back appearing fuller on one side than the other. If the contour of the back, viewed at eye level, not looking downwards from above, appears identical on either side it is safe to say that the asymmetry which is seen in the standing position does not involve the spine to any extent that would interfere with the training, providing—and this is an important reservation—that movements of the hips are equally free on both sides, such tests as *grands battements*, *développés*, *arabesques* forming a useful criterion. It would be unwise to teach a child if there is any doubt whatever on the result of this test without a further orthopaedic opinion.

The back which shows some asymmetry with no corresponding spinal abnormality to account for it is very common and is considered by modern orthopaedic surgeons to be a failure of the muscles on either side of the spine which are responsible for the maintenance of posture to receive and respond equally to the nerve impulses connecting the brain to the muscles, a failure which may be due to fatigue, too rapid growth or even emotional instability. Certainly one finds this condition in children with excitable and sensitive temperaments and very often with an insecure background. In such there is a steady improvement as training proceeds and the whole poise of the body is stabilised. By the third year if such a child is training seriously there will be nothing left to see—but not necessarily before that time.

If the asymmetry is due to some slight difference in the length of the legs, it will not disappear, but the body adapts and the mature dancer is able to manage the small problems it creates. They are not of sufficient consequence to cause the rejection of a talented child with an otherwise suitable physique, but there may be a limit to final brilliant accomplishment with this handicap.

There are many other formations of the back which must be considered, the spine which has a longer than normal curve backward in the mid-region leaving a short lumbar hollow and sharp angle as it meets the sacrum, a difficult back to alter, since "pulling the tail under" does not plane out the hollow, but only increases the rounding above; the too flat back with a sharp angle at the base and often combined with large hips and stiffness of movement in the lower back, and one in which pulling the tail under is apt to produce a curve backward in the lumbar region. This last irregularity, a spine which shows a curve backward in the lumbar region in place of the normal hollow, was at one time a rarity. Now one finds it too often and the question comes to

Fig. 51.   THE APPEARANCE OF AN ASYMMETRICAL SPINE OF THE TYPE WHICH OFTEN HAS NO STRUCTURAL BASIS

Note uneven level of ears and shoulder line and apparent displacement of the body to the left.

mind as to whether it is the result of too much interference with posture in young children. The injunction often heard, "pull the tail under", may be a necessary correction for a very hollow backed child, but may succeed in reversing the hollow in a flexible child not in need of such a correction. The

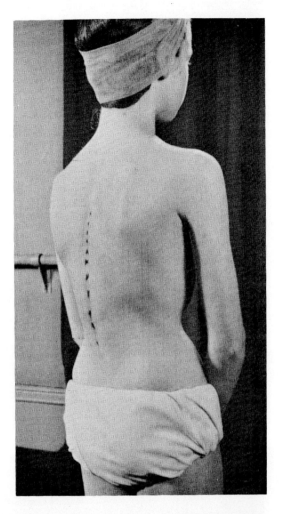

Fig. 52. LUMBAR CURVE
REVERSED
(Compare Fig. 15A)

point is worth considering, for the result is a weak back which tires quickly even in everyday life. We have no record as yet as to what will happen to such in a few years' time, but we would hazard a guess that they will feature amongst the slipped discs and sacro-iliac strains if taking up a stage career. Figure 52 shows such a back at 12 years old. In a tunic the posture appears good. Lesser degrees are also found, often with some sinking in between the shoulders, but still passing as good stance when clothed.

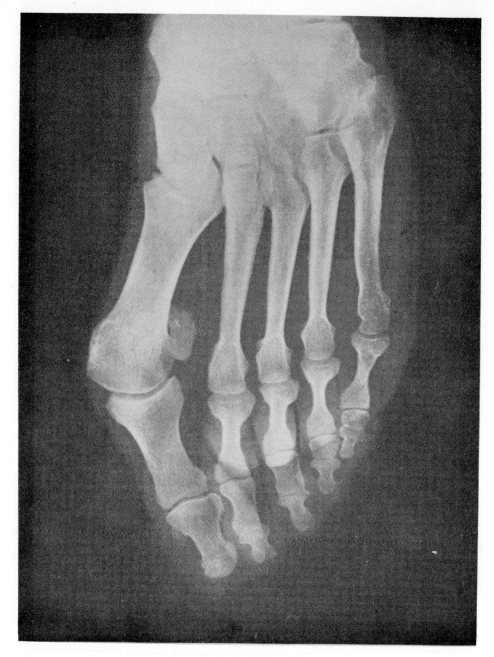

Fig. 53. *HALLUX VALGUS* IN A NON-DANCER SHOWING
DISPLACEMENT OF BIG TOE
Note sesamoid bone (normal) under 1st metatarsal.

9. CAN ANYTHING BE DONE FOR ENLARGED BIG TOE JOINTS?

Very little, and that is why prevention is so important. Much has already been said on prevention in the foregoing chapters—the correct holding of the foot on the floor; the avoiding of rolling and *sickling-out* (see Fig. 33); delaying of "*pointe*" work until the whole body is sufficiently trained; well-fitting shoes with low or moderate heels. Then there are types of feet which should never be given any ballet at all, however simple—the foot with an over-flexible big toe; the highly arched foot, too soft and flexible, with long metatarsals and toes; the very tightly-knit foot with little or no arch—and so on.

The enlarged big-toe joint, technically known as *Hallux valgus*, is really a dislocation of the joint, with subsequent inflammation of the joint surfaces. The foot broadens owing to the increased space between the 1st and 2nd metatarsals. Even if the bones could be replaced by fixation or manipulation, they will not remain so and unfortunately once the condition has arisen it tends to progress, whilst pressure from the shoe causes a painful bursa on the outside of the joint.

In the *very* early stages, electrical stimulation of the abductor muscles of the big toe may help to draw it back into place, as does the wearing of a contrivance to preserve the alignment of the toe. It is also important to keep the joint flexible. An advanced case can only be treated by a surgeon, and even then the results are by no means uniformly successful.

There is another trouble which is quite commonly found, known as *Hallux*

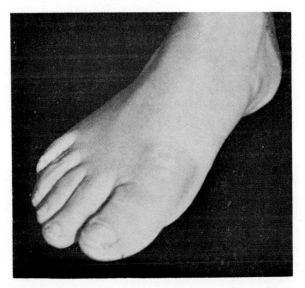

Fig. 54. THE FOOT OF A WELL-KNOWN DANCER
AFTER 20 YEARS OF POINTE WORK

A strong type of foot with moderately high arch
which wears well.

rigidus, in which there is no displacement of the joint, but there is severe inflammation which produces rigidity. This is more painful and more disabling to a dancer than *Hallux valgus*. Surgical correction however can be more satisfactory than in the case of *Hallux valgus*.

Both these conditions are extraordinarily common in people who have done no dancing. They are often hereditary or rheumatic, but probably the biggest single factor in producing them is wrong footwear (for which reason they are found more frequently in women than men). The over use of the foot (including standing) in any occupation will bring trouble upon the owner if there is any predisposition to it.

10. IN WHAT POSITION SHOULD *grands pliés* BE GIVEN FIRST?

Whether the class should begin in 2nd or 1st pos. is a question upon which even famous teachers are not agreed. In older students it is probably not of great importance. In beginners, however, the 2nd pos. is simpler and mistakes are more easily noted by the teacher. By simpler is implied not easier, but less complicated from the point of view of muscle and joint action. The body is in a more stable position than in 1st pos. The common fault of "rolling" and the falling inwards of the knees is quickly detected, and the tendency to hollow the back more easily checked. The temptation to sink downwards by force of gravity without using the resistance of the thigh muscles is less when the heels are firmly on the ground. So that, although *plié* in 2nd is a more powerful exercise than in 1st, it is easier to perform correctly in the earlier stages.

There is another reason in favour of beginning in 2nd pos., viz.—the stretch on the inner thigh muscles is more immediate and greater than in 1st. This stretch includes the large blood vessels, arteries and veins that run down the thigh towards the inner side. The circulation is therefore quickly increased. On a cold day very few *pliés* in 2nd performed strongly and accurately with the right degree of outward pressure of the knees and with pressure on the floor with the feet, will result in a glow of warmth beginning in the thighs and gradually spreading over the whole body. Every dancer knows the value of "warming up", and for this reason alone it may be preferable to begin the class with *pliés* in 2nd pos.

11. HOW FAR DOWN SHOULD THE DANCER GO IN A *grand plié?*

The depth to which *grands pliés* can be taken depends upon four things:
1. The strength of the spine.
2. The flexibility of the hip joints.
3. The elasticity of the muscles on the inner side of the thigh.
4. The length of the Achilles tendon of the leg.
   All these factors are equally important.

Pliés, especially when done in 2nd pos., gradually loosen the hip joints so that the knees can be pressed out fully and the movement taken until the thighs are parallel to the floor, whilst the back is erect and the knees over the centre of the foot. This is an advanced stage. To arrive at it may take years of steady work if the hips are not naturally flexible. Until then, the movement should be taken only as far as correct execution is possible.

One rarely finds permanently stiff muscles on the inner side of the thigh. With steady work they will stretch to the required length.

The Achilles tendon, by which the calf muscles are attached to the heel, may limit the degree of movement at the ankle joint and therefore prevent the performing of a full *plié*. It is not a very flexible structure and force should not be used to stretch it, or inflammation in the tendon and even damage to the lower fibres of the calf muscle may result. In time it usually yields sufficiently, but occasionally one meets a really short tendon and must then accept the limitation it imposes. Nowadays many schools precede all *grands pliés* with two or three *demi-pliés*, a useful procedure for ensuring correct execution. (See also Question 6.)

12. SHOULD THERE BE ANY PAUSE BETWEEN THE SINKING AND RISING MOVEMENT IN *grands pliés?*

Definitely not. Whether the pupil is able to take a full plié, or is limited by any of the factors mentioned in the last question, the movement should be smooth throughout and the rise begin without pause. If there is any "sitting", the ligaments of the knee are kept on the stretch and the strain on the joint is very considerable.

Ligaments can be safely stretched during the course of a movement because surrounding muscles then safeguard the joint, but in "sitting" they are made to take the weight of the body without any such safeguarding and the knees may thus be permanently weakened. Faulty pliés may easily be the cause of a slipping cartilage at a later date.

13. AT WHAT STAGES SHOULD THE *grand plié* IN THE 4TH POS. BE INTRODUCED?

This is a relatively advanced exercise. If it is used too early it will be incorrectly performed, with a twist of the pelvis and rolling of the back foot. It is easier to create errors than to correct them. *Demi-plié* in this position may form a useful introduction. In the full *plié* the lower back and hip muscles must be strong and the inner muscles of the back leg must be capable of a full stretch or the knee will fall inwards, and with it, the foot. On the forward leg, certain muscles of the hip which have a dual action cannot work at full strength in keeping the knee out-turned, since they are partly engaged in preventing the pelvis from twisting. It is therefore a movement requiring both strength to overcome the difficulty and a fine kinaesthetic sense, i.e. muscular awareness, which one cannot expect in the elementary stages of training, but which is developed to a high degree as training proceeds. It is neither beneficial nor advisable to try to cut short the process of acquiring this awareness, which should come gradually as the result of the pupil's experience of the effort required to perform each movement, a subjective process which the teacher can assist, but not impose upon the learner.

14. WHAT EXERCISES SHOULD FOLLOW *pliés?* I HAVE ALWAYS TAKEN *battement tendu* AT THIS POINT, BUT THE CECCHETTI METHOD GIVES *grand battement.*

Pliés are designed, among other things, to loosen the hip and knee joints and to warm up the limbs in preparation for the exercises to follow. The foot, however, does not share fully in the warming up since it moves in a relatively small range of flexion with no extension to follow, and in actual fact the circulation is compressed at the ankle joint rather than increased. To complete both the loosening of the ankle joint and the flow of blood through the foot to the toes, the use of *battement tendu* rather than *grand battement* would seem the logical choice to follow pliés.

15. IN THE *battement tendu,* DO YOU THINK IT HARMFUL TO PUT WEIGHT ON THE TOES AS THE FOOT IS EXTENDED?

Perhaps "harmful" is too strong a word, but it is definitely undesirable. In doing so there is a slight but definite movement towards "rolling" on the *supporting* foot, or if that is avoided, a slight tilting of the pelvis upward on the working side occurs. Small errors of this kind repeated many times become habits which interfere with the perfect placing of the body.

From the point of the foot itself it is likely to lead to flexibility without strength, always a handicap in advance work. This is especially likely to happen *if the toes are curled* in an attempt to force the instep into the appearance of a higher arch than in fact usually exists. Curling the toes inhibits the action of the small muscles which pass along the sole of the foot, but do not take any part in the movement of the ankle joint. These muscles are immensely important in holding the arch strongly. When they contract strongly, the foot actually becomes smaller. This can be seen in balancing movements, and it is due to the training of these muscles that the foot of the dancer does sometimes become smaller as training proceeds. It is therefore very important that the habit of curling the toes in *battement tendu* or any other exercise should be checked as early as possible.

16. MANY STANDARD EXERCISES START WITH A *pirouette* FROM A *grand plié.* DOES THIS PRESENT DANGERS FROM AN ANATOMICAL POINT?

Most advanced exercises are safe for the advanced student, but ill-advised, if not dangerous, if taken too early. A *pirouette* from a *grand plié* presupposes that the executant has complete control over the knee joint. If taken with the weight on the inner side of the knee, it can have the same results as a badly executed Telemark turn in skiing, viz., strain on the inner or medial ligament of the knee. The strain may be slight only, but repeated often it can lead to weakness or even disability.

17. IN ORDER TO KEEP THE THIGH TO THE SIDE IN A *développé*, A CERTAIN AMOUNT OF TIPPING OF THE PELVIS IS NECESSARY. TO WHAT EXTENT SHOULD THIS BE PERMITTED?

The mechanics of *développés* in any position involve both the hip joint and the spine (see Chapter V). Taken to the side, there is a good degree of movement in the hip itself, especially when there is a good turn-out. Taken to the back, as in *grand battement*, the limit is soon reached. After that the spine bends laterally or forward, as the case may be, to increase the height of the leg, and the pelvis tips accordingly. If this bending and tilting is permitted in the early stages the hip will never gain its fullest flexibility, and even more important, the back will not strengthen, for it is in holding upright against the inclination to tilt that valuable muscle work is given to the spinal muscles throughout their whole length. It is this added strength that makes it possible for the advanced pupil to take a high *développé* with perfect style and placing.

18. DO YOU BELIEVE IN LIMBERING EXERCISES? IF SO, WHEN SHOULD THEY BE GIVEN—AT THE END OF BARRE WORK OR IN THE CENTRE.

There is probably no more controversial question than that of the value of limbering and perhaps nothing that is taught with less discrimination. There are also many forms of limbering, from the occasional stretching exercise at the barre to a whole series of exercises in sitting and lying positions, forming a large part of the lesson.

Ballet technique is a highly scientific system of movement designed to create strength, flexibility and endurance. These three MUST progress simultaneously. Too great flexibility will be acquired at the expense of strength if short cuts are used to obtain it, and it is in this that the danger of limbering lies. As an adjunct to the barre, and given only to those who need it, certain stretching exercises may be useful, but they should be given only when the body is fully warmed up and within the style of the classical technique. The dancer who has not the control that is built up by the slow and steady development acquired by years of side and centre practice will never achieve ballerina perfection.

19. A MATTER OF GREAT CONCERN IS THE DANGER OF OVER-DEVELOPING THE LEGS OF OUR DANCERS. IN AMERICA, AS I IMAGINE IN ENGLAND, THERE ARE MANY STUDENTS WHO WILL NEVER BECOME PROFESSIONAL DANCERS, AND IT IS INDEED A TRAGEDY WHEN THEIR LEGS BECOME BULKY. FROM THE AUDIENCE'S VIEWPOINT IT IS ALMOST AS GREAT A TRAGEDY WHEN PROFESSIONAL DANCERS HAVE KNOTTY MUSCLES. ARE THERE ANY EXERCISES WHICH SHOULD BE AVOIDED?

It does seem that there is a type of physique that remains slim and streamlined no matter how much exercise is taken, and another that will thicken no matter how little. Very little research seems to have been done on this problem, but from the point-of-view of ballet, as in other activities, the first safeguard against bulk is that the muscles should be used to their fullest in both directions.

In practice this means that a contraction should always be followed by a stretch. Much of the barre work provides for this. For example, *développés* in front, which contract the muscles on the front of the thigh, are followed by *développés* behind, which stretch them, and so with *grands battements* and many other movements. There is, however, another factor which is equally important, namely, relaxation of the muscles which have been tightened, and this is provided for by the momentary return of the weight on to both feet between such movements as are performed on one foot. In that moment, the muscle fibres relax. This is therefore a very important part of execution which does not always receive sufficient emphasis. If the weight is kept too long on the supporting foot alone, the muscles will become too hard; if the working leg is kept in a state of contraction without the momentary release, there will also be bulk, unwanted and ugly. It needs a watchful eye on the part of the teacher to check the tendency to evade this transference of weight on to both feet, however transient.

20. DO YOU BELIEVE THAT LONG *adagio* EXERCISES TEND TO ENLARGE THE LEGS? WHAT ABOUT JUMPS?

It is mainly at the barre that there is danger of increasing the size of muscles, and as we have said in the last question, this is minimized by very correct performance. The lower leg muscles get their stretch after contraction by the pull on the lower fibres in the *demi-plié*, and this should be taught correctly from the beginning. Jumps will not increase muscle bulk if performed correctly, beginning and ending with as full a *demi-plié* as possible. In the same way, long *adagios* are harmless providing they are so designed that there is continuous movement. Lengthy holding is more likely to create bulk than any amount of smooth movement.

21. HOW CAN TENSION IN THE PUPIL BE CORRECTED?

There is nothing more contagious than tension. A teacher who is over-anxious herself will also produce tension in her pupils. One sometimes sees a teacher giving out an enormous amount of energy in voice and gesture, contracting her own face and neck muscles, and at the same time exhorting her pupils to relax! The real answer to this question lies in the art of teaching, the ability to stimulate the lazy pupil, to calm the too ambitious or nervous child and to maintain a relaxed yet authoritative presence in conducting the class.

22. HOW SHOULD THE FOOT BE USED IN WALKING?

Ballet dancers have the reputation for walking badly. It is probably undeserved on the whole, but doubtless the habit of turning outwards during working hours persists in the feet, if not checked, in the relatively few remaining hours of the day. Undoubtedly there will be a lack of smooth graceful walking if the feet do not point in the direction of the walker, but even more important is the fact that, when the feet are turned out in walking, the weight of the body is received on the inner side of the foot, and at each step there is a push off the ground by the ball of the big toe with the foot abducted and everted, in fact "rolled". Children especially should be taught the importance of straight foot walking, for they are apt to dream of the stage and translate its conventions into the movements of everyday life.

23. SHOULD THERE BE ANY DIFFERENCE BETWEEN THE TRAINING OF BOYS AND GIRLS?

The author is indebted to Claude Newman for this reply, the conclusions reached as the result of many years as a dancer, and as teacher of the boys of the Royal Ballet School, and The Royal Academy of Dancing.

"There should be a marked contrast between the male and female dancer, and therefore there must be some difference in their training. The approach for the male should be more athletic in type, work being directed toward developing strength, virility and elevation. For junior boys the emphasis should not be placed on turning out, nor should the leg be raised too high, as strength then often disappears and the weight becomes misplaced. Head movements should be definite, the face turned rather than the neck bent.

Senior boys should have special exercises for back and arms to increase their strength for lifts. Some boys may benefit from the addition of other forms of physical training in order to increase their courage and attack for specifically male steps. In general, boys should work in a broader manner than girls, and whenever possible should be taught in company with other boys by a male teacher."

FROM THE AUTHOR TO THE READER
CAN YOU ANSWER THE FOLLOWING?

Draw a line representing the normal curves of the spine. Explain how these curves are altered by the tilt of the pelvis.

What is the effect of breathing on the chest wall and spine?

For what reasons might a child have difficulty in taking a good 5th position of the arms (Cecchetti 5th *en haut*)?

In which exercises is the straightening of the knee of special importance and why?

What are the bony points of the foot which can be seen? By which special point would you recognise a rolling foot? What is the effect of rolling?

How should the weight of the body be distributed on the foot in standing?

What is the importance of using the pressure of the foot on the floor in such exercises as battements tendus and battements frappés?

How do you recognise knock knees? How do they differ from the normal? What effect does this condition have on the feet? What precautions would you take in teaching a child with a marked degree of knock knees?

What is the danger of turning the feet out too much in beginners and why?

What is the danger of too early "pointe" work?

For what reasons would you refuse to teach a child with anything abnormal in the structure of the spine without medical sanction? What signs would lead you to suspect any abnormality?

List of Books Recommended

Art Students Anatomy, by Edmond Ferris. (Lippincott, Philadelphia.)

Anatomy, Physiology, Pathology and Bacteriology for Students of Physiotherapy, Occupational Therapy and Gymnastics, by C. F. V. Smout, M.D., M.R.C.S., L.R.C.P., R. J. S. McDowall, M.D., D.Sc., M.R.C.P., F.R.C.P.(E), and B. T. Davis, M.B., C.H.B., M.C. (Path). (Edward Arnold Ltd.)

Anatomy and Physiology for Physical Training Instructors in Royal Air Force, (H.M. Stationery Office).

Anatomy for Artists, by Eugene Wolff, M.B., F.R.C.S. (H. K. Lewis Ltd.)

Human Figure Drawing and Anatomy, by A. Gladstone Jackson. (Elliot Right Way Books).